Growing Up
In Minby

Growing up in Minby

by

Lloyd H. Person

*In memory of my parents,
Oscar and Alma Person,
Saskatchewan pioneers,
who worked very hard and
died too young*

CONTENTS

PREFACE

PERSON'S PEOPLE

by Hugh Hood

The number of possible human persons is infinite and
infinitely various, and we cherish every individual person
as unique, utterly unlike every other person who has
existed, is living now, or will perhaps come to be born.
The special, irreplaceable value of the person is an axiom
of civilization; we are the children of God; nobody's
experience can be duplicated. And therefore everyone is
uniquely valuable because he or she has a special witness
to give, a particular window opening on history.

The number of possible human groups is likewise
transfinite, though there must be at least two persons to a
group. The forms of societies are almost as special, almost
as valuable as human souls, because of their range of
possibility. We cherish the forms of societies because
they are like human beings in their uniqueness and their
special witness to life. A group of human beings who agree
to live together in a certain place, in a way which is
appropriate to that place, create together a form of existence which is nearly as much worth preserving as one's
self. For societies are quasi-personal. They can know,
love, grow, decline, and die as people do, and they have a
type of immortality; they live in history or they ought to.
Every social form should be preserved in some way, in the
movies, in books. The wish to preserve and memorialize
the forms of social life — the family album, the dynastic
novel, the genealogies compiled by county historians, the
work of a Balzac, a Dreiser, a Hugh MacLennan, all grow
out of our common need to record, preserve, make a
picture of ways of community living. These ways are
always peaceful and usually loving, the ways of the good
family. They are *familiar*. "Our Father which art in
Heaven," the beginning of the Lord's Prayer states the

source of this need to celebrate loving human action. We always try to capture for our descendants the good and happy peace of our forefathers. History is a recollection of Divine Being, and perhaps the fundamental motive of the storyteller, the narrator. We don't just need to memorialize past societies, we *ought* to do this. To write history, to tell the story of our forebears, is to perform an act of piety, a deeply moral act.

Lloyd Person has made it the work of his maturity to memorialize the small town he calls "Minby," Swedish for "my town." In doing this he has carried out an action of fundamental literary and human value. Starting from his own life in Aylesbury, Saskatchewan, and concentrating on the end of the nineteen-twenties and the beginning of the thirties — crucial years in all of modern living — Mr. Person has recorded the minutest details of daily living, and more than this has given an intensely artistic illumination of them, in a way reminiscent of the shining, super-real sculptures of his friend Joe Fafard. There is in Lloyd Person's work the same loving attention to detail, the identical care for the people described, as in the Fafard ceramic portraits — the strict literalness and the striking eccentricity blended into unforgettable perceptions of real, individually-lived lives. Lloyd Person's "Minby" is a place unlike any other. We are not meant to universalize it as we read. It isn't the same as Aylesbury or Craik or Delisle or Pense. Not the same at all. It is *this* place with *these* people in it and no others. Sometimes you hear it said that regional literature only becomes great when it becomes universal, and this is taken to mean "general," referring to any similar region.

That is quite wrong. The way to make regional writing, like Lloyd's chronicle of "Minby" life, great and finally valuable, is to insist on the specialness, the uniqueness of what happens in your own town, almost your own family, almost indeed your own self. The more personal — or Personal — the writing, the more real it becomes.

This is what is meant by the phrase "the concrete universal," and the analogy with certain basic notions of Christianity is clear.

So "Minby" isn't quite Aylesbury or Craik, but an artist's imagined realization of his town, a genuine literary creation, no doubt derived from the experience of life in Aylesbury in 1928, 1929, and 1930, feeding on the town's life — the peculiarities of some of the townsfolk, their predictabilities and even more their unpredictabilities, requiring Aylesbury to exist, but leading a life independent of the real town, just as the imagined towns of Mark Twain and Stephen Leacock remain more real than those which equipped them to write, Hannibal, Orillia.

"Minby" existed in the full flower of its familiar reality from the beginning of the present century to the middle nineteen-sixties, say two generations in all, not a long span of time. Now the place is almost uninhabited. The buildings remain but most of the people have left; where once there were six or seven elevators in operation, now there are two, or one, or none. The gas stations have closed, or will close soon; there isn't the business to support them. Most striking of all is the absence of children; you don't hear the young voices through the daytime. There's no school in "Minby" any more; another town was awarded the district comprehensive school. There's no blacksmith in town, naturally. You'd look a long time to find a horse there.

A young boy used to be able to tell the time of day by the sound of a labouring locomotive on the long steep grade up the bank of a big coulee; now he listens in vain. The four daily local trains, two up and two down, were discontinued one by one. Now there is no local rail traffic. A highway used to run through the outskirts of town. The last big new four-lane highway bypasses "Minby," leaving it a mile to one side of its route. The driver in his speeding car sees small ghost town after town drift across the big screen of his car windows, like a series of forlorn mirages, as he makes the run from Regina to Saskatoon at a speed inconceivable in 1930. He can't see any people in the fields or on the streets of the towns; there are none to see. All over Canada the countryside is becoming depopulated. By the year 2000, we are told, only five percent of the population of Canada will live in the country or in small towns. The rest of us will be living in medium-to-large cities. The next quarter-century will be a good time to buy country real-estate at sacrifice prices, if that's where you want to live.

It would be senseless to look for any reversal of the drift towards total urbanization of our lives in the foreseeable future, and idle to complain about it. If it hadn't been for Lloyd Person's great industry and imagination (the present volume forms only a small part of the whole of his work), in another generation the life that went on in "Minby" in all its intricate network of behavior would have been lost to us, would have disappeared into an awful void. When we think of that — the possibility of the absolute disappearance of these rich narratives, so that nothing whatsoever remained of them — archaeology in reverse, so to speak — we can see what we owe to the imaginative social historian, a precious inheritance.

Lloyd Person tells us here that there was once a pretty sizeable number of folks — over two hundred of them — who lived together in this particular way, without violence or criminality, in a society which performed beautifully. It was a good way to live. And now it is gone.

Montreal
June 8, 1974

MINBY — 1928

MY DAD, Ingve Viggo, one of the Minby pioneers, was proud to be able to say he had arrived in 'three, which he said, like the other first-comers, with a sort of offhand pride — instead of saying "nineteen three." Dad had homesteaded in the Minby district, just outside the village, choosing his quarter section right next to Montague's. Dad's original quarter also adjoined what forever after became known as the "Old Pringle Place" and this was very near the *original* site of Minby.

When after three years the town was moved west a mile, so was the cemetery, one body dug up and symbolically transferred to the new location west of the *new* Minby, the others left where they were. For years thereafter whoever farmed the "Old Pringle Place" — since the first cemetery was located on a corner of it — cut an extra furrow into God's five little acres until it finally disappeared. It seemed tacitly agreed by the long succession of tenants that the ground should be plowed up and put to use — but not all at once.

Although Dad settled in Minby and homesteaded in the district, he actually spent most of the first two years in Missenden, nine miles up the line, where he and Mr. Nilsson, an Old Country friend, operated Missenden's first blacksmith shop. It was only when Minby's site was definitively settled that Dad gave up his first homestead — it was extremely poor land anyway — dissolved partnership in Missenden, and operated the shop in Minby on a full-time basis instead of the one or two days a week he had done when he worked in Missenden. Over the sliding front door was the big sign which he himself painted and which he was to freshen up every year thereafter colorfully proclaiming: "Ingve VIGGO, your Blacksmith and Woodworker since 1903." In 1928, then, this sign had been up exactly one quarter of a century.

My Dad never gave up his idea of having a farm, however. Mr. Gottselig was a Minby pioneer too, one of the very first, arriving a few years ahead of my Dad. When he decided to buy more land, he and Dad bought a section together — Mr. Gottselig would farm Dad's half for him.

The first twenty years of my life were spent in Minby, so it will be those early impressions which will be recounted here. In summer Minby was hot and dry, yellow-brown or straw-colored rather than green, for there was little grass anywhere. The only trees and hedges the village boasted were those that my Dad, Ingve Viggo, planted and they looked dusty most of the time.

I remember the buggies and wagons drawn by horses more than I do the automobiles in the Minby of 1928, although it had its share of cars when I was a kid: we weren't that far behind the times! We weren't behind the times at all — Minby boasted everything obtainable on credit. But when I was growing up, horse-drawn transportation was preponderant. Practically all of the grain was still hauled by horses and wagons, very few farmers having trucks.

Only two or three of the Minby women were bold enough to try driving their husband's car. Mrs. "Red" Blaine was one, and she drove their Maxwell as belligerently as she did everything else. She always seemed spoiling for trouble, even behind the steering wheel, as if she were looking for someone to run into or bite, for Mrs. Blaine never just barked.

Mrs. Tischler was another of these early Amazons — she handled their old Model T much better than Mr. Tischler did, but then she was credited with doing just about everything better than he. Wherever she went, she generally went alone; when "Dad" Tischler *did* accompany her, however, he looked like an alert little fox terrier disporting himself behind a slow-moving, obese English bull. The fact was she looked like a bulldog but, unlike Mrs. Blaine, Mrs. Tischler was a lovable woman with a gruff, friendly bark and no bite at all.

Mrs. Tischler was also the music teacher, and when she drove that old Ford she drove it in exactly the same way that she played the piano — with the accelerator, like the loud pedal, pressed to the floor. Miraculously enough she never had an accident. She only ceased to be a menace on the roads when, after one long winter, she got too stout to get behind the wheel.

In 1928 most women were still driving a horse and buggy, coming in to town in the afternoon with an egg crate and their freshly churned butter up in front with them, a coal oil can, and a few plowshares to be sharpened stuck in the back. If the women didn't make and sell their butter themselves or if they didn't trade it in on groceries at one of the local stores, then they would have one or two cans of cream with them which they dropped off at the CPR depot to be shipped.

There were hitching posts or hitching rings at regular intervals along Main Street where they could leave their buggies, but I recall mainly those in front of the Pool Room and Stewart's Store. The horses could also be tied up to the telephone poles lining the back alley parallel to the main drag, or driven in behind the different places of business. What we called the back alley was in reality — as the archives of Minby are my witness — King Street.

A blurred first memory of Minby was the CPR station. Since Dad's property was almost on the southern boundary of the village — only the Lobbs, the School, the Kaschls and Hopkinses were farther out than we — and since the depot or station was north of the tracks, entirely obscured by the elevators and the coal sheds,

I didn't get to see it up close until I was a few years old. I still hear my parents warning Kalle and Greta, my older brother and sister, never to venture down to that part of town, they were to stay on *this* side of the tracks, *this* side of Main Street. The same warnings were repeated to me when I got old enough, and to my younger sister and brothers after me.

It must have been a Sunday when I went with Dad that first time, because Sundays were the only days he was free. It was also in the dead of a bitter cold winter. He had pulled me down on the handsleigh and we were to go on down to the valley afterwards.

We arrived at the station just in time to see the big passenger train pull in from the north, and though I had Dad beside me and was holding his hand, I was paralyzed with fear as the big locomotive slowly pulled past, three-quarters obscured by the hissing steam escaping around it. When it came to an impatient stop — for no train stopped longer than necessary in Minby — it was to unload a couple of Minbyites, Dad Tischler and Reg Hopkins, who had been "up North" hunting. From an open flatcar that made up part of this composite train, their kill — a couple of huge moose frozen stiff — was also dumped on to the station platform.

I knew those moose were dead and couldn't hurt me, but I was scared to death of them anyway, especially when Dad lifted me up on top of one to have my picture taken. The head of the larger one was mounted and proudly displayed in the Pool Room and Barber Shop thereafter. Mr. Grant was one of a long succession of proprietors of that Pool Hall and a lover of big game; he was furious one day when he saw that some practical joker had cut off the moose's bell.

It is hard to believe that in 1928 when I was a youngster there was enough business in Minby to maintain two passenger trains a day each way, two in opposite directions in the afternoon, the same two after midnight, about twelve hours later, when they went back.They used to meet in Missenden, the first village north, about halfway between the two big cities.

In addition to passenger trains there were freight trains. Saturday morning was their favorite time to shunt, and when I was in Saturday School getting my surfeit of catechism the two dreary years Reverend Kreuz was with us, I would squirm and fidget as I jealously wondered who was in *my* place up in the cab with the engineer and fireman. They were *my* friends. One of the two, the engineer I think, had a little sideline: he would buy all the fresh mushrooms we could bring him after a rainy day. In the first place, if he was likely to meet a passenger train, he knew he could dispose of them to the chef in the dining car; failing that he had a ready market for them in the city.

The same engineer could actually have his engine blow gigantic smoke rings, although it may have been by sheer luck that it happened when he had an audience of admiring youngsters. He could make the black monster blow rings from that smoke stack, shooting out what looked like thin platinum hoops which we followed with our eyes until they disappeared into the thin air.

It was also by chance that on two occasions a big locomotive lost a very essential connecting rod pin from its steam-making mechanism as it labored up the north curve. It happened the first time one spring before I was born. My Dad in his shop almost a mile away could hear that there was something the matter and years afterwards he used to tell my brother Kalle and me how he jumped into his car that day and sped up to the disabled engine. What he suspected had happened, had indeed happened, and he was able in a couple of hours' time to help the engineer on his way by improvising a repair. Evidently because of the heavy green vegetation along the railway track at the time the train crew hadn't been able to find the missing pin.

Late that same fall when Dad and Mom were out for a Sunday stroll along the railway tracks Dad spotted the pin. In the fall now, with the vegetation dried up, it was plainly visible. It had had such a heavy coating of grease that it hadn't suffered the least damage from the rain. Dad took the big pin home with him, cleaned it and greased it up once more to protect it, and then he set it up on a shelf by the forge.

Many years passed . . .

And then one fall day as I was helping my Dad in the shop, another heavily laden freight was gasping as it labored up the same steep incline. How often had Dad thought back on that earlier incident? How often had he glanced up at that pin? It was, he said, as if he expected to hear the same telltale miss of steam again. This day when he *did* hear the identical symptoms, he reached up for the pin, grabbed his toolbox, shouted, "Come on, Wally!" and we were off. In ten minutes we were up beside the stranded engine.

"Who the hell are you?" asked the puzzled engineer who was worriedly contemplating the extent of his misfortune.

"Oh I'm the Minby blacksmith," Dad said as casually as he could, but I could see how pleased he was with himself. "I could hear you were having a little trouble and thought I better hurry out. Wally, you wipe off that big pin real clean while the engineer here and the fireman help me lift this arm back up where it belongs."

In less than half an hour the incredulous engineer was back in his cab once more slowly making for Missenden and points north . . . It was worthy of Ripley's *Believe it or not.* The two exactly similar accidents had taken place in approximately the same spot, fifteen years apart; only the engineer was different. It was the same sort of engine, if indeed not exactly the same one, for we used to see the identical ones on our line week after week, year after year, and their numbers were as familiar to me as the names of the engineers who drove them.

The Minby station — it has been closed now for years and up for sale — served another purpose in addition to its foreordained use, more poetical this time. "Lud" Oberholz, the agent, was a bachelor. Through work for the day which was at supper time, he would remove his CPR cap, lock up, and head across the tracks to the Twentieth Century Cafe where he took his meals; from there he went on down to Minby's social center (the Pool Room and Barber Shop). Now locking up, winter and summer alike, meant closing up everything with lock and key with the single exception of the waiting room door. In winter Lud always had a nice fire going for the comfort of the rare passenger who might be taking or getting off the night train. He generally left the door of the big stove half open to act as a check. That also provided what light there was. . . . Although the benches weren't the most comfortable ones in the village, more than one Minby romance was furthered, some even hastened, by this convenient meeting place.

My Dad's blacksmith shop was *not* the center of Minby, but it *was* the focal point of my young existence. It was one of the first businesses erected in town, located on the corner of Queen Street and Argyle. Who else but the village clerk and perhaps my Dad would have known that Argyle Street was the dirt road coming in from Culbertson to the south? It crossed the track and continued on, first west three-quarters of a mile, then north to Missenden.

It is unlikely that Dad sought a business advantage in setting up shop where he did. He was probably just showing his usual consideration for others by keeping the noise of his triphammer as far away as he could from any houses. Our own, for example, was in the same block, but as far east as possible, with the chicken house, some garden and the trees in between.

There had once been a big house immediately to the north of my Dad's shop. It, along with a barn and still another house over two blocks away in another part of town, had belonged to Richard Cantelon. These three rather widely scattered buildings all burned down before I was born; but I saw the yawning basements of the two houses with the rusting furnaces and miscellaneous junk in them as well as the foundation of the barn up near Bethel Church. Since his buildings were not adjacent to one another, Mr. Cantelon was unable to convince the insurance company that his fires that night had been accidental.

Richard Cantelon's one son Hedley now occupied the parental farm just outside of Minby. Quite unaware of what was really involved in the public school system at the time, but possessed with an inordinately high opinion of himself and an even more pressing feeling of civic duty, he early aspired to the chairmanship of the School Board, a position he felt no one in the district better qualified to assume than he. Enough of the local ratepayers shared this opinion, voting accordingly, to keep him in that lofty office for thirty years. Knowing virtually nothing about everthing Hedley was thus able to cast an unprejudiced tie-breaking vote in the event of a deadlock. His decisions were as unreasoned, as unpredictable and as open to chance as the flip of a coin. Whether asked to or not, Hedley Cantelon would never have been able to bring forth more than half of the proverbial two cents' worth. For three decades then, in such hands as his the destinies of the young Minbyites — mine included — reposed.

Minby's Old Hotel (a misnomer in the sense that it had only been standing fifteen years) was a huge, ramshackle, jerry-built structure that should have been condemned before it ever opened its doors in 1913. It had been closed as a hotel in 1918 but one big room was used occasionally for public events for five or six years.

I have a vague recollection of being taken to at least one show in what was proudly called the Ball Room of the Old Hotel. It was a traveling stage representation of *Uncle Tom's Cabin,* deservedly the last of its kind to come to Minby, for when it reached our village the entire cast, ticket seller and propman included, numbered but five — three men, a blond (Eva), and a huge rheumatic Saint Bernard with sore feet. Of that grand production all I *really* remember — other than the prolonged Transfiguration of Eva ("I'm coming, Uncle Tom!") — is the dog as it was simultaneously enticed by Uncle Tom holding a huge chunk of meat offstage at the left, and prodded in the rear by someone off to the right to get out on stage and pursue the slave across the ice. The painted backdrop depicting ice floes had all the realism that the floes onstage — make-believe covered cartons — did *not*.

The same Ball Room was the only dance floor Minby could boast until the Community Hall was built in the early twenties. Mrs. Tischler often contributed her services as pianist. The Minbyites waited years for the new building, dancing dangerously in this rickety firetrap which *un*settled so badly the very first year it was built that the front steps and main front doors were *never* used. "Old Jack" Smythe claimed that those double doors, as long as they were left jammed shut, were all that kept the second floor on the north side from coming down. I was told too — although I was never old enough at the time to verify this for myself — that the fire escape for those upstairs rooms consisted of a rope fastened to a leg of the bed in each room, long enough to reach out of the window and down to the ground.

Across the street and west of the Old Hotel was another shambles which went under the name of Gene's Garage and Tire Repair. After filling one garage with cars he had dismantled and motors he hadn't been able to get back together, Gene Dempsey was starting over again in what had been an implement agency. When a vehicle miscarried, there was one of two things the intrepid owner could do: try fixing it himself (using Gene's tools — Gene was very obliging, knowing they would sooner or later have to come to him) or call on Gene himself who was only too happy to administer the *coup de grâce* although that was never really his intention.

When you stood at the Old Hotel corner and looked east, you were looking right down Main Street. Main Street differed from the north-south road only in these respects: it was wider, harder and dustier when it wasn't raining, and dirtier, muddier and ruttier when it was, since all the elevator traffic passed that way. The new Pool elevator was the first in line of half a dozen inverted hemorrhoids sticking up against the prairie horizon. Those elevators formed a line between Main Street itself and the CPR tracks, the space between them in turn taken up with the coal sheds. Since elevators and elevator men are part and parcel of every prairie town, their *modus operandi* demands particular attention.

The other elevator men, before Belette's arrival, had been good friends and co-operated with each other, visiting back and forth from office to office when they didn't have a customer to wait on; or you'd see them walk off together to the Pool Room for a friendly game of snooker; they even helped one another load when the pressure was on in one elevator and they could be spared from their own. Without this sort of help, Max Harrison, with his asthma, would hardly have survived. They helped one another move boxcars. They politely left one another's old-established customers alone. They lived and let live, forming the friendly little fraternity of Minby Grain Buyers although they never designated themselves as such.

Walt Belette threw a monkey wrench into all this in 1928, his first year in Minby, as soon as the farmers started to haul grain. With the construction of the new elevator, Belette's was now the second on Main Street. All grain tanks and trucks therefor had to pass his to go to any of the other four elevators, unless they took the back way in, which hardly anyone did. He had a commanding position to see everything that went on as he sat by the open window of his office; and justifying his every action with the fact that he was a newcomer to Minby and had to get started — blissfully glossing over the fact that he had his predecessor's customers already coming to him — he was in and out of his elevator, up and down the steps from his office, like a gopher in and out of its hole, when a wagon hauling grain came by. He would slither down the steps, his peaked cap pulled down over his eyes, would jump up on the side of the moving wagon, reach in for a handful of grain, make the farmer an offer of a better grade than it merited, simply to get him to change his mind and come into his elevator, knowing the man was going to drive past anyway.

The other buyers regarded this as unfair and unethical. Of course they could have adopted similar tactics to a more limited extent, depending on their own elevator's position in line, but none would stoop to such a practice. They had all been buying grain for years, they had all been giving their customers the best possible grades; they knew, then, as the farmers themselves should have known, that if Walt Belette went them one and sometimes two grades better than the stuff was worth, he would have to have some mighty good grain to mix with it, or resort to some *other* stratagem once he had the wagon over his scales.

Immediately east of the Old Hotel on the corner was a still older claptrap of a hotel, dirty and square and brown, long ago demoted to the status of boarding house since the travelers no longer stayed there. The proprietress or her girl could be seen any day of the week emptying chamber pails out of the only second-story window the place boasted on the west side, disproving time and again the sneering rumor that she hadn't a pot for the proverbial purpose, nor a window to throw it out. Happily, the few years the adjacent Old Hotel was in operation, its Dining Hall never faced that way.

"Barney" Grant's Pool Hall and Barber Shop came next, a long narrow wood structure with a treacherously sagging roof. Maybe the arrangement of the tables precluded the installation of center supporting posts when the shell was put up. The hall was only slightly wider than a standard Brunswick billiard table was long, just enough wider in fact to allow the snooker sharks to get comfortably around the ends of the tables.

Then came Stewart's Store, the Cafe, and directly across the street from it the Municipal Building, rebaptized the "old" Municipal Building when it became vacant. That was two years earlier, in 1926, when it had been decided that the municipal affairs could be more centrally handled from Culbertson to the south of us.

East of it was the building everyone referred to as the Drug Store. Drug Store it had *never* really been, for the first proprietor had never been qualified to fill a prescription. It only earned that appellation because for the few years that Dr. Grenz lived in Minby, a wide assortment of patent medicines had been kept. Prescriptions had to be phoned or mailed to the city to be attended to.

The same building now housed the telephone central of the two local lines. Mrs. Barry, the first telephone operator Minby had, started as a young lass in her teens when the exchange was put in, and she *still* enjoyed being called the "hello" *girl* although she was well into her thirties. She could overhear and enjoy any of the conversations passing through her central during the day, keeping abreast of the local scandal, not one whit of which was any spicier than the pages from her own Thousand and One Nights. Busy as she was at the switchboard, she could still get up and make a sale of a scribbler, a chocolate bar, a newpaper or a magazine between "Number?"'s.

Mrs. Barry didn't carry more than two or three hundred dollars' worth of stock all told, patent medicines, newspapers, confectionery included. Nor at the very most could her confectionery account have been worth more than sixty or seventy dollars a month, yet the travelers of the four principal wholesale companies spent far more time at her place vying for it than they did at Stewart's or Kovacz's whose grocery accounts were fully fifteen times as large. Rumor had it that the more persistent salesmen, the really eager beavers, came back after hours to deliver their final sales pitch. . . . In this year of our Lord 1928 "Scoop" Lowe from Bath and Scottgate's seemed to have a smug bulge in getting her order, but "Marsh" Crabtree, a dark horse, had been showing signs recently of getting on the inside track.

Then came the Post Office, the front door of which was open twelve to eighteen hours a day depending on the season. There was a cluster of people every day at one o'clock with the wicket down while they waited for their mail and the city newspapers to be sorted. Busiest and most important of all the people there each day was "Old Scott" McEachern. He seldom got anything, but then one never knew. . . . There were seldom as many at four o'clock when the afternoon train went back, except on Fridays, of course, when *The Missenden Thunderbolt* and *The Western Producer* came down to the Minby subscribers.

"Fweeny" Watchler, behind the wicket of the Post Office, was as industrious in cumulating any other benefits to be pocketed as was her husband, whose principal occupation was telephone linesman but who found time to sell hail and life insurance as well as to deliver the mail bags from the trains to the Post Office. Her big job, of course, was sorting the mail which her husband brought. She was busy again the first fifteen or twenty minutes after the wicket was open when she handed out parcels or gave the mail to those who had no box.

Since Mrs. Watchler had to be in the Post Office before and after the mail was sorted *anyway,* she carried out minor little bookkeeping chores. They didn't pay much individually, but for the time and effort involved, the remuneration was quite respectable. Everything she did, she did in the name of her husband, whose name, scarcely legible when he signed it, always appeared at the bottom as "secretary," "treasurer" or both. The contrast between her handwriting and his on a report could be likened to a Grade One pupil signing his name under his teacher's.

Minby had two telephone lines, one on each side of the valley. Although there was only one central, Mrs. Barry, the "hello" girl — in whose old Drug Store building the central was located — just assumed that the small extra duties of secretary for the two lines would go on being hers as they had been in the past. The two hundred dollars a year that she received from them was an appreciable percentage of her yearly income. Mrs. Watchler could and did do this job, offering to do it for one hundred and fifty.

"Your cigaret money, dear," she was supposed to have said to Mr. Watchler.

Mr. Watchler was quite often heard to say, "No — I don't want all the insurance business, just ninety-five per cent of it!" His wife had taught him that catchy little line; it was the same little formula she used so successfully, laughing hypocritically behind the wicket of the Post Office like a lynx in a cage, to pass it off as the joke it wasn't.

Then Kovacz's — now *there* was a store! It was on the corner of Duke and Main. It was primarily one long narrow building extending the full block from Main to King, that is, to the back alley. The front half of this immense building had counters and shelves down each side. Standing inside the store, facing west, you were looking at Kovacz's tremendous stock of dry goods; facing east, you were gazing at Kovacz's equally impressive array of groceries.

Back in the shadows stood the big red coffee grinder; it was so high, and with such a big wheel on it with a crank, that Louis or I — when I helped him — had to stand on a fair-sized stool to turn it. The south half of this building housed the Kovacz family with Louis, my age, coming exactly midway between his six sisters. The lean-to east of the store, also facing Main Street, was Mr. Kovacz's Butcher Shop.

Perhaps it was true that Mr. Kovacz had different prices for his customers as I heard many say. If, while picking up a meat purchase for Mom, I *once* heard Mrs. Kovacz ask her husband how much an article was, I heard her ask half a dozen times. Her questions to him always varied, depending on the item and the quantity involved. His reply, cleaver poised in midair while he asked his question, was always the same: "Who is it?" And not until he heard who it was did he give the price.

Behind the butcher shop annex the fenced-in, L-shaped area contained a heterogeneous inventory: old cardboard cartons, apple boxes, lengths of old lumber and other junk. There was always some manner of poultry running loose inside. Chicken wire was stretched from the ground to a height of twelve feet or more, and within would be anywhere from half a dozen to ten dozen crates of live chickens and roosters raucously cackling.

"Kass" Komos might be in that enclosure too, having come in from his little farm for the day. One by one, Kass, covered with blood and feathers, would extricate the struggling birds from a crate, hang them up by the two legs, stick his razor-sharp knife into the squawking open beak, and before the blood really started spurting out, he had half the feathers off. No way of telling from Kass's expressionless face if he enjoyed his job; but it was one way — a sure way — for him to earn an extra dollar, since Mr. Kovacz could get no one else to do the work for him.

Across Duke Street, also facing Main Street, was Müllers' Hotel or the "New" Hotel as it was most usually called to distinguish it from the others. It was, in fact, built the year before with a reputation already unsurpassed by any of the other hotels on the line. Still further east, strung out facing Main Street and the elevators, were Alec's shoemaker shop and half a dozen small houses, each with its still smaller outhouse backed up to the lane, the owners of which, for the most part, were the elevator companies themselves. They had built them for their own buyers who were now occupying them.

There were three short streets, at right angles to Main, which, if you consulted the village records, bore such high-sounding names as Athol, Duke, and Connaught; but since not one of these side streets extended more than two blocks, their names were never necessary. Besides, everyone made his daily trip to the Post Office for the mail, although it meant having to ask Mrs. Watchler for it if he didn't have a box. The Lobb sisters, across the road from my Dad's shop, exaggerated when they used the street name as part of their address, along with the name of their big house, "Manwaring Manor."

I should mention Dr. Grenz's old house on one of the side streets. He lived in it only a short time before moving to Missenden, yet his name stuck with it ever after because he had been the original occupant — just as the "Old Pringle Place" was always designated by that name, regardless of who happened to be the current tenant.

Dr. Grenz built a sumptuous palace after he made his move to Missenden which would indicate that he had only been camping in our town. He probably would have burned that first house to the ground when he left, had he ever suspected that Reverend Kreuz would one day be giving religious instruction from its living room. Dr. Grenz, like Einer Haugen, was an atheist. "But he's such a good doctor!" exclaimed in a chorus the two Lobb sisters who worshipped him *anyway,* marveling incredulously at their own broadmindedness and the fact that atheism and good medicine should go hand in hand. Maybe Dr. Grenz was such a good medico because, being an atheist, he left *nothing* to prayer.

Little old Minby boasted no less than three wells. They were within a radius of 200 yards, yet three more different sources of water in such a small area would have been hard to find. Old Jack Smythe was first and foremost a farmer, but he was also the well digger. He made an excellent supplementary living those first years following the well witchers around Minby and Missenden. He said he would never say anything unfavorable about a dowser, adding, with a wink, "not even the *bad* ones . . ." because he had made too much money after them.

The closest well to Dad's blacksmith shop was called the village well, or the Windmill, probably because it happened to be the first one dug. It was the one well relatively close to the Livery Barn and was mildly alkali. Some people used this alkali water for drinking and cooking purposes simply because it came from the well closest to their homes. Mr. Stewart, one of the general storekeepers, wouldn't use anything but, claiming that without it he would have been "plugged up long ago." He said many a time, to his men and women customers alike, that it was only "that water that kep' a hole" through him.

The next pump was alkali too, but of so high concentration that it was unfit for consumption of any kind. Dad had the bottom half of a 45-gallon steel drum standing between his anvil and forge which he kept full of this water and into it he plunged the plowshares to cool them. He had still another long narrow wooden container, more like a trough, with six to eight inches of this same water in it for cooling and shrinking wagon tires when he had one to set. Perhaps the bitterness of the water added something to the acridity of the smoke and steam as the rim burned into the wood.

The alkali content of the water was so high that you could see, with the water in it at rest, the irregular white high-water line on this trough. One could not see this without being instantly reminded of one of Minby's boys, Willie Schurk. Willie was a chronic pants-wetter, so slow in realizing when he had to go that it was usually too late when he went. He soaked his pants years after he had started school, and day after day we could see the same telltale rings around his crotch when the pants dried. Until this deplorable malady left him, he was never called anything else but "Alkali" Willie, and thereafter a much more grown-up, better fitting nickname, "Horse-face" Schurk.

The third well, a few steps from Bethel Tabernacle, miraculously enough gave excellent water. This was the "good" well.

Every winter, by Christmas time, the so-called village well had so much ice around it from the water that had been spilled, or from the leftover water that had been dumped from the trough so it wouldn't freeze and split, that one risked fracturing a leg coming to use it. The telltale signs of the different shades of yellow in the ice showed that some of the farmers, nay, the very villagers themselves who used the water for drinking purposes, thought the little pumphouse similar enough to an outdoor toilet to be used as one — certainly for urinating around it. Maybe the extreme cold weather in winter, and the absence of a ready handful of grass precluded its use for the *other* purpose as well.

Each year, around freeze-up time, some member of the village council would see to it that a little sign was put up in the pumphouse with flowery circumlocutions forbidding its use as a comfort station. To no avail . . . Had they simply printed in big block letters "Don't piss here!" they might have got their message across — at least to those who could read and understand English even if they ignored the basic rules of hygiene.

The Viggos were the first family in Minby with electric lights. As a small, small lad I remember Dad unpacking sixteen big glass batteries in our basement which he set up on two large shelves not too far from the hot-air furnace where they wouldn't freeze.

In the next room stood the Fairbanks-Morse engine which ran the 32-volt generator. I clearly remember when Dad turned on an electric light for the first time — perhaps because, like the First Book of Moses, there was something miraculous about it: Dad turned on a switch to make light, and, as it says in Genesis, there was light — instantly. I cannot recall, on the other hand, when we used the coal oil lamps. Having always seen them *then,* from birth on, they just hadn't impressed me. Now with electric lights they were left filled with kerosene and set aside on a shelf out of the way, in reserve against a power failure that never took place.

Unfortunately the engine had to be going at night to give adequate light, the very time when Mom wanted it quietest. The lights were not only brightest with the engine running, but with the belt running directly from the flywheel to the generator, there was a visible pulsating increase in the intensity of the light with each power stroke of the engine. We all got used to that however, and, in time, to the racket of the engine.

By far the majority of the business places as well as all the private homes except our own relied on a Coleman gas lamp or coal oil lamps. Mr. Kovacz had the most advanced gas system for miles around, with a 25-gallon tank outside his store with its own built-in pump to force the fuel to the individual burners. These hung just below the ceiling of his store and were so high up he had to light them from a candle on the end of a six-foot length of binder whip.

Now a quick trip to Missenden, the first town north, the better to understand what Minby *didn't* have and how it affected our little village's history. Missenden beat Minby to the draw with the first "movies" in the district. It is quite true that not very many Minbyites regularly went to the shows at Missenden, but those "not very many" from our town, plus another bunch from Culbertson and from the other surrounding towns all contributed to make Missenden's Lyceum Theater a paying business.

Those people who went to Missenden were, in a smaller sense, just as symptomatic of our already dying village as was Dr. Grenz who had left a few years before; as was the Dominion Bank that closed in 1927 to be followed by the Standard Bank this year just twelve months after; as were three of the four machine agencies now closed, one transferred to Culbertson, the others to Missenden. So every time Dad loaded up the eight Viggos — nine counting Angèle when she was still with us — plus at least two Kaschls to see Ken Maynard or Charlie Chaplin, and, if we were lucky, an *Our Gang* comedy, it meant that three or four dollars left Minby to swell the coffers of Missenden and make it a more thriving little town than our own.

Perhaps, too, it was the flip of a coin that decided Jas. A. Caxton to start his newspaper, the weekly *Thunderbolt,* in Missenden instead of in Minby or Culbertson. We subscribed to *The Missenden Thunderbolt* from the day the first copy left the press, and it and *The Western Producer* came down every week, Friday afternoon, on the four o'clock train. I wonder why Dad subscribed to it because I rarely saw him look at it. If he did, it was only to check the format of his current advertisement and to see where Mr. Caxton had put it.

The Missenden Thunderbolt was a four-sheet, eight-page weekly. No one in our house ever read pages 2, 3, 6 and 7 which weren't even set up in Missenden. Most of the other pages were filled with advertisements that we paid no attention to either. We all read the local news, however, not to see what had happened the week before, but to check if the Lobb sisters had remembered to put it in. We generally knew about these events anyhow, for being a close friend of Mrs. Haugen we heard about most things *before* they happened. But the really good, juicy tidbits weren't printed anyway . . . We'd get them from Angèle.

Angèle thought there was nothing like *The Missenden Thunderbolt;* she read the obituaries first and would consider the week's edition had somehow failed if there wasn't at least one good one in it. Only then would she read the "Lost and Found" and the "Local

Happenings." She admired the Lobb girls' mastery of the King's English. Regularly, but never more than once a year — the Lobb girls never overdid anything — the one or the other sister would mention, in writing up one of the fowl suppers, that "the tables fairly groaned under the weight of the tempting viands"; regularly, too, at least once a year, generally in January or February, three months or so after the Special Treatment accorded the Fowl Supper, they would write up one of the more successful dances, concluding how "everyone tripped the light fantastic until the wee sma' hours of morning."

It is true that Angèle didn't always understand what she read, she was still learning English, but she was nevertheless aware of and impressed by the prodigious learning that was background to the flowery literary phrases the Lobb girls used. How often she wished that she'd be able to write English like that some day!

Minby wasn't a representative cross section of the district as a whole. We had one Jewish household, the Kovacz family running the Dry Goods and Grocery Store. It has already been indicated that Mr. Kovacz had the only good butcher shop in town. Müllers in the New Hotel were German. There were the Chinese in the Twentieth Century Cafe. There was my Dad of Scandinavian background and he ran the Blacksmith Shop. It seemed that just about all the other businesses in the village *at the start* (Hawthorne, Stewart, Maynard . . .), all the elevators (Whitmore, Elliott, Smales, Harrison, Renfrew . . .), the Post Office, the Coal Yards (until "Uncle" Martin came), the Livery Barn, until *farbror* (father's brother) Hasse took over, were run by people of British extraction.

The Minby farmers didn't reflect the village breakdown, however. Perhaps as few as a fifth of them were of old Canadian stock from "down East" or from England. Three-fifths were fresh imports from Europe (Germany and Russia principally), the other fifth coming from the States. Even in 1928, however, a number of the Americans were either absentee landlords with their farms rented out, or they just came up in the spring to put the crop in and, like the birds, headed south at the first sign of cold weather.

The Americans, more than anyone else, had been the bold entrepreneurs, and were responsible for the big steamers rusting in the fields around Minby, huge power plants that were as good as obsolete when I was born. When, one fall, Old Jack Smythe's huge steamer came through Minby pulling a 42″ separator, a hayrack filled with straw to feed it, a water tank, a couple of wagons, two cook cars and a string of bundle wagons, everyone was out to see the procession go by: it was the last . . .

Gangs of harvesters used to come from "down East" to help with the threshing, but even before we left Minby that was beginning to be a thing of the past. Those little migrations ceased completely at the beginning of the thirties when nothing grew. But again I'm getting ahead of myself.

Already by 1928 then, when Minby's first quarter century of existence was coming to a close, several buildings which had appeared as solid as the Rock of Gibraltar only a few years before were standing idle or had been converted to some other use. The brick Dominion Bank, three machine agencies' buildings in scattered parts of town, the Lodge "shack," the Municipal Office, and of course the Old Hotel were already relics of Minby's heyday and its present decline.

When Dad left Missenden twenty-three years earlier to open his business full-time in Minby, could he possibly have imagined that something like two decades later, where all things had once been more or less equally promising, Missenden to the north and Culbertson to the south were to "go ahead" while Minby "went back"?

Missenden and Culbertson liked to flex their muscles, boldly bragging as they called themselves *towns*. They had a condescending way, too, of saying "Oh — Min - by . . . !" Tragically enough they were living in a sort of fool's paradise, for in 1928 Missenden and Culbertson were "going back" too — they just didn't know it!

This, then, is a short description of the sort of community into which I was born, the sort of community in which I and how many thousands of others spent the first part of our lives, for fifty years ago the Prairies were much more rural than they are today, the "country mice" far outnumbering their city brethren. I loved Minby, we *all* loved our Minby, but obviously not enough to stay. Now, five decades later, when we nostalgically think of going back, often there is nothing, or pitifully little, to go back to.

"Minby," of course, is a composite of many vanishing or already vanished prairie villages. You'll find it nowhere or everywhere on the prairie maps. The following sketches are a mixture of fact and fiction, mostly fiction. "Minby" just happens to be two Swedish words, *min* and *by,* meaning "my" and "village" respectively. Might I not just as well — for all you former ruralites, for all you former "Minbyites" — have called it "Dinby" — *your* town, instead?

REVEREND ALVAR AND BIBLE SCHOOL

THIS YEAR, this summer we had Bible School for the first time. Six long, long dreary weeks of it. There were just enough young children in our congregation to warrant bringing a student minister to Minby for the summer. So for these six long weeks, six long days a week, from eight in the morning until four in the afternoon we were catching up on the religious instruction we had missed without a permanent resident minister. If I admitted for a time a few years later that there might possibly be a heaven, it may partly have been because I was sure there was a hell: I had had forty-two days of it that summer.

The adults, too, made up for the church services they had missed because on Sunday the enthusiastic young pastor held services twice, first in the morning — the regular Bethel congregation held its church service at two in the afternoon — and again in the evening when "God's Sanctuary," as Reverend Alvar just loved to call Bethel Tabernacle, was once more free. The men, my father among them, decided Reverend Alvar was working himself much too hard, and after the third Sunday only morning services were held.

Four of the six Viggo children were of Bible School age; there were three Bachs, Erik Haugen and his brother; several Guschlbaurs; the two Milford girls; Ronnie Müller, plus another few from families who didn't even belong to our church. The parents — so the mothers said — were so-o-o glad of the chance to have their children "get instruction." Perhaps they were just relieved to have them out of the way and supervised for the summer. There was also, last but not least, Willie Schurk.

Willie was mentioned last because he was last in every-thing.

What all did we do? To start with there were such hilariously exciting things as learning hymns and Bible verses by heart, and the Lord's Prayer, of course, if we didn't already know it. Reverend Alvar thought there was nothing like knowing it in another language so we learned it in Norwegian, Swedish, and German. We learned the Beatitudes and certain of the Psalms. We learned the books of the Bible by heart and doubly blessed was he who could say them backwards as well as for-wards, since it helped to win prizes.

Yes! We could win prizes! The first ten minutes every morning as well as the first ten every afternoon were devoted to competitions when row was pitted against row, or the boys against the girls, where pages were furiously turned to see who could be first in finding a certain verse in the Holy Scriptures. This was "Know Your Bible!" One of the merits of "Know Your Bible" was that as long as I was busy trying to find a particular Bible passage, my mind was taken off my itching eczema. I had never before had this skin disease but in the third week of Bible School it declared itself on my arms with a vengeance and was with me for two solid years thereaf-ter.

We were taught, along with certain rudiments of catechism, what the shortest verse in the Bible was, and which was the longest; we were expected to know which books of the Bible were the shortest and longest, impor-tant facts which we dared not confuse or forget; we were awarded Wall Mottoes of dubious artistic value, but of certain commercial worth, since dozens of them were distributed in the course of the six weeks we were assembled; there were enough passed around that summer to have shingled the roof of the old school *and* the little Bethel Sanctuary. We also won celluloid Book

Marks with dark purple flowers and bright green leaves, many of which had the same verses on them as the wall mottoes. We were awarded Old Testaments and New Testaments (mostly New) and individual Gospels from the New Testament, and my three soft-covered Gospels of St. Matthew alone are mute testimony of the excellent memory I had then.

I wasn't many days finding out that Reverend Alvar's competitions meant absolutely nothing, since he somehow found a way to pile his awards on to even the most recalcitrant in the class. Willie Schurk, the prize dunce in Public School, continued his unbroken record in Bible School too. Does this prove some kind of correlation between the spiritual and the profane? He only had to burst into tears when the minister asked him to recite the lesson for the day. Reverend Alvar would comfort him, pat him on the head for trying, give him his Testament, Wall Motto, Bookmark or Gospel and go on to the next in the class. And, head down, looking sideways over towards me from behind his hand, "Horseface" Schurk would smirk or grin, showing how smart even the most stupid can be.

For a while Reverend Alvar asked me to take Willie out behind the school to go over some of the passages, prayers or hymns that we all had to learn. He had to be prompted on the very first line of the Lord's Prayer which sounded something like "Are far we chart niven holler be thy name." This was conclusive proof for me, proof I didn't need, really, that poor Willie hadn't the faintest idea what the Lord's Prayer was all about. If he could recite it in German, word perfect—although even then he probably didn't know exactly what it was all about, it was because he had heard it all his life at home, three times a day, where it was recited as grace before breakfast, dinner, and supper.

If I say that Willie did not understand such elementary things as the Lord's Prayer, I must admit that much if not *most* of what I learned by rote was over my head too. When we recited the 23rd Psalm and said "The Lord is my shepherd I shall not want" I was a good many days fussing and puzzling over that line, since the sentence seemed to be incomplete. When we "want" or don't "want," it is something we want or don't want, I thought, and in my befuddled young mind I remember once trying to put in a relative pronoun to complete the sentence. I said "The Lord is my shepherd whom I shall not want" but my reason or common sense, startled out of a deep comfortable sleep, rushed to my rescue; of course that couldn't possibly be what was meant.

Nor was I surely the first kid ever to question how a land could be beautiful that was "flowing with milk and honey." Wouldn't it be awful to live in a place where, I imagined, one could only get around in rubber boots? I had a perfectly vivid recollection as a preschooler, not too many years before, of being helplessly mired in the muddy road just south of our house, and of having to be lifted bodily out of it. Wouldn't honey be much stickier and suckier than mud?

Bible School had a negative effect on me since it occupied me with nothing interesting. There was always in the back of my mind the irritating haunting thought of *what we could be doing instead.* My father, a hardworking, industrious individual, planned and saved to give us kids what he thought was indispensable for our happiness: education, material things and experiences he himself had never had as a child. Until the period of Bible School just over had we ever wasted a summer like this? At a time when not too many people went camping, my Dad always found time to take the family to a resort, leaving his helper alone to run the shop for a few days. Sometimes Mom and us kids stayed out a fortnight or more with Dad only coming out weekends. Many a summer we went to one of the lakes for an enjoyable holiday or north into the bush country to camp. This was paradise for Mom and Dad since it reminded them very much of Sweden or what they so nostalgically referred to as "home" or "the Old Country."

I can never recall missing the Provincial Exhibition before this ill-fated Summer Bible School episode either, and this had always meant a four-day safari, since it took one day to get to our destination, two days to take everything in, and the final twenty-four hours to pack up and make that long hundred-mile trip home again; this journey we made with our big touring car, trailer and camping equipment, throwing up our tent on our arrival right alongside the Indians and their teepees, all of which were among the features we had come so far to see. Perhaps we were as much a spectacle for them as they for us . . .

All this, then, I could think back on with nostalgia while sitting in the stifling heat of the Old Stone School the month of July just over, scratching my itching arms, trying to keep awake, trying to be interested in something that bored me to tears. Nor is this an idle image because as old as I was, far beyond the age of tears — I was ten — and certainly not one given to tears anyway, I was on the verge of bawling this morning when I was particularly fed up with Reverend Alvar, Bible verses and catechism. I pleaded with my mother to let me stay home *just once*. But she was adamant. Angèle, our hired girl, had definite ideas about discipline and catechism too. But she would know and understand, I thought.

"Can't I, Angèle?" I asked, turning to her for support.

Angèle would have let me, had she thought she could have gotten away with it. Mom just laughed and said, "Angèle's not your mother!"

The odd respite behind the school when I was to help Willie Schurk learn his lines turned into little sessions where we "played knife." Dull as playing knife was, it was more interesting than trying to teach Willie anything. Even such forbidden fruit as this childish pastime had little to offer a prying mind after fifteen or twenty minutes, particularly when I knew, as did "Alkali" Willie, who didn't learn his lines out behind the school either, that there was no danger whatever of Reverend Alvar coming out and catching us at play. Willie had two knives which he used, one of which, a "Premium Stock Knife," was his special favorite. When he told me it was his big brother's "cuttin' knife" and explained what *that* was, then I realized there were vast virgin areas in my sum of knowledge which even an imbecile like Willie could illuminate for me.

Sometimes we played "threshing machine." But to play threshing machine properly required foresight and a belly full of water. We would unbutton our flies, take out our "blowers" and see who could "shoot straw" the farthest and highest. Sometimes if we didn't have "straw" we would play threshing machine anyway. Willie, who wasn't called "Horseface" for nothing, had something else beside his profile and buck teeth in common with a horse . . .

My interest perked up just a bit in the last week or two of Bible School. Erik Haugen, though more than two years older than I, could have passed for my younger brother since he was only about half my size. He was the oldest in the entire Bible class, yet he was almost the smallest of all. Mom always said that that was because "the poor boy doesn't get enough milk." Mom had extremely rigid ideas about the importance of milk in a growing child's diet.

Erik was a good deal smarter than I was too. He had received a special reference Bible from his aunt when she learned that he was "reading for the pastor." When it dawned upon Erik what Potiphar's wife *really* wanted when she commanded Joseph to "lie with" her, he eagerly started little excursions all of his own, following any references in his Bible to what he called "the good parts." He found lots of them, which really isn't so strange since they were all in the "Good Book."

It must be said that Erik's Bible was an excellent one in that respect. The biblical expert who had compiled these particular *renvois* had a mind that operated in exactly the same fashion as Erik's and my own. Before the last week of Summer School was over, we had become past masters at reading 'twixt the lines, and with the help of the appropriate references we had precise ideas of what went on in Sodom and Gomorrah before those cities were destroyed by brimstone and fire. We read such entertaining passages as Genesis 38 and it was undoubtedly at that time that we learned that harlots, whores and prostitutes were all sisters under the skin. We read and like hardened old lechers savored the incestuous story of Lot and his two daughters. If wine can provoke the desire and also take away the performance, as Shakespeare so aptly puts it, then Lot's two girls must have known *exactly* when to put the cork back into the bottle.

But even this literary activity soon lost its charm for Erik and me. Like playing knife, or threshing machine, reading these lusty episodes, albeit couched in conservative Bible English, wasn't forbidden fruit either, since they were to be found in the first Bible Erik and I could put our hands on; and Bibles, Testaments and Gospels had been distributed wholesale that summer! Had any of the adults even remotely suspected what was in the Holy Scriptures that kept Erik and me so attentive—that is to say this last week when we *were* attentive (Erik had had all he wanted of Bible School too)—they might have supervised our reading a little more closely.

Even if these more exciting passages were in the Bible, and even if all our instruction was centered around this Book, I knew I shouldn't get caught reading these daring chapters by Reverend Alvar or by my parents. As a matter of fact Mom was observing me one day, quite unbeknownst. When she heard me snicker, apparently enjoying myself, she was sure I couldn't be doing my lesson. When she asked if I didn't have some sort of joke book concealed inside of the Bible, she tacitly acknowledged that when we studied our catechism it wasn't for any pleasure to be derived from it.

At long last, then, when these six weeks were finally by, I felt as if I were waking up after a long nightmare. It hadn't really lasted twenty years like Rip Van Winkle's sleep, it just *seemed* that long. The fact that I was free as a breeze until regular school started should have made me rejoice and it did, but only mildly. The six weeks I had lost, the interesting things I had missed, and the fact that it was so late in the year, too late for Dad to take us for our usual holiday—all hung like a pall over the fortnight that remained before school started again. But, however bad things had been, I murmured to myself philosophically, they could always have been worse. What if we had had to spend *every* summer like this?

I didn't even remotely suspect what the future had in store for me.

A few days were to elapse before I learned we would be having our own permanent pastor, one living right in Minby.

BUILDING THE NEW POOL

THE ELEVATOR gang arrived late, in the summer of 1928. Yes, in 1928 Minby was sure it was holding its own, in spite of the bank closing the year before. And wasn't a new school being built? Wasn't another elevator going up? . . . a second brand-new Pool Elevator right alongside the first? Wouldn't that mean another family moving into town? Indeed, the incorrigible Minby optimists said that our village was even "going ahead"!

When Bible School was over I could spend some time down at the elevator site. The noisy presence of that gang of Swedes down by the tracks could be heard all over Minby.

Teams with scrapers were leveling off a big patch of ground by the tracks. It seemed they were doing a lot of work for nothing, because once they got the ground smooth, they started in again with the same horses and scrapers to make a great big hole. This, of course, was for the grain pit, and the big steel pit itself which weighed many tons had been unloaded a day or two before on the old wood platform parallel to the spur, and was now the congregating point of every kid in the village. Here it would remain for a few more days until moved down into the hole which was still under excavation.

Upside down, its shiny black surface warmed by the sun, this steel pit-to-be made an excellent sliding board for us kids. Willie Schurk, incapable of remembering two consecutive lines of catechism in Bible School, took great delight now in standing on top of the pit and proclaiming to all the world the only secular lines he knew by heart:

"I'm the king of the castle
and youse are dirty rascals!"

and "Sissy" Kaschl, the town tomboy, the only girl in

a family of twelve, would come up and rattle off provoca-
tively:

"Here I stand, ragged and dirty,
When the boys come to kiss me,
I run like a turkey . . ."

These Swedes were the merriest, noisiest, swear-
ingest, snuff-suckingest, profanest bunch of individuals
that had been in Minby in a long, long time — probably
since the last elevator was built. The majority of such
traveling construction gangs had been Swedish. Being
Scandinavian, I had seen Scandinavians all my life, but
most of those had been long-faced and sober like our
minister. Even Mr. Haugen, Erik's dad, a Norwegian
and therefore Scandinavian, was on the serious side when
he wasn't drinking. *These* Swedes, on the other hand,
had obviously just reached Canada a few months or
perhaps the year before because they spoke very little
English. There was one exception, their manager, the
only really elderly one in the gang, and he spoke English
without an accent. I had learned Swedish at home and
made a hit with the gang right away. Thus when a syrup
pail of cold drinking water was to be fetched from the
Minby well, I was the one to get it. And getting that
pail meant earning a nickel!

I was impatient, of course, to see the elevator go
up. It was supposed to be higher, ten feet higher than
the highest one we already had in Minby, higher than
any elevator in Missenden even! But as long as the pit
had to be dug and foundations poured, it just seemed
that my Swedish friends weren't doing anything. They
were, of course, being employed very efficiently. One
group was cutting huge piles of two-by-fours and two-by-
sixes into the proper lengths and stacking them accordingly. Once the gang of them started building in earnest
a few days later, they literally devoured these pre-cut

lengths at the rate of one a minute as the elevator two-inched its way upwards.

Another half-dozen Swedes were standing in line in front of a gigantic pile of siding. Spread evenly apart, brush in hand, a pinch of snuff stuck in one or *both* sides of their mouths like pocket gophers, they were sloshing the first coat of red paint on to the elevator before it was even off the ground! Bertil, the shortest and youngest of them all, became my special friend. Golden hair stuck out from all sides under his white painter's cap. The red on his cheeks wasn't paint, but the "ruddy tint of health" like I had been reading about in *Dickens in Camp*. He may have been only twenty or so at the time, but to me, half his age, he was quite a man. Even he used snuff. When he gave me a quarter to go to the Pool Room to get him a can of *snus,* as he called it, he always let me keep the dime change. The first time I made such a purchase, Mr. Grant asked me without cracking a smile, if I wasn't a little too young to "chew."

I earned many a nickel and dime running errands for the Swedes. But even this rather unexpected good fortune was augmented in a fantastic manner, particularly on Saturday nights. The Swedes had pitched two big tents on the north side of the tracks quite close to the elevator site. They had quickly knocked together temporary double-tiered bunks which they set up all around the inside of the larger of the two tents; these bunks they filled with straw over which they spread a blanket and this arrangement served as their mattress.

The other tent was their kitchen and dining room. They had their own Swedish cook with them, who spent fully half his time making meatballs or mixing pancake batter. Behind a rudimentary canvas curtain they would completely strip after each day's work, washing themselves clean, dousing one another with buckets of water from the tank that had been awarming in the afternoon sun.

Even more rudimentary than the Swedes' sleeping quarters and dining facilities was their "John"; this was nothing but a narrow rather deep slit trench, above which was a planed-off length of four-by-six, about two feet above ground level. Nothing more . . . On this they perched philosophically, sometimes two at a time, concealed certainly from the local citizens outside their compound, but well in view of each other from within.

My Swedish greeting the first day was an Open Sesame which allowed me to go anywhere in their little camp. What was my amazement the second day to behold under the bunks an accumulation of several dozen empty beer bottles! From then on, my first errand was to take our little hand wagon and cart these "dead soldiers" home. The fifteen cents a dozen I could get from them represented money in quantities unknown to me up until then. If I sometimes came away emptyhanded during the week, my haul early Sunday morning always made up for it.

On the last Saturday night they were in Minby, these Swedes had a real plastering bee and finished the inside of the office building alongside the elevator which was also to house the big engine; then they all got gloriously plastered themselves.

I rubbed my hands with an anticipatory gleam in my eye, counting my chickens, alas, before they hatched. My bonanza the next morning was the smallest I had ever had, inversely proportional to the hangovers the Swedes were nursing. Empty whisky bottles, unlike beer bottles — in spite of the higher cost of what had been their contents — weren't worth a cent a hundred. The gang had a couple of days to sober up on while making their move. Was that why they had abandoned their plebeian beer for something stronger?

The last Sunday afternoon they knocked down their camp, and late that evening the whole gang and all their equipment, my good friend Bertil too, were gone, picked up by a passing freight. The next day only the filled-in trench that had marked the "John," the tramped down area where they had walked around in and out of the tents, and the now wind-scattered straw that had served as their mattresses, indicated where they had camped. I would have given everything I possessed to have gone along with them.

My hopes were built up for a time when we heard that the Federal was putting on a 20,000-bushel extension, and I hoped my Swedes would be back again. But they didn't come back. And my friend Bertil who had promised to write? It took a whole year's impatient wait to convince me that his letter wouldn't come either.

"OLD JACK" SMYTHE

JACK SMYTHE came into town that week with the first load of grain for the year. Jack was my oldest friend. For twenty-three years, with the exception of the 1914-1918 years when he was in uniform, "Old Jack" had been the first to get his threshing outfit in order, *some* of his grain harvested and the first load of wheat hauled in to the elevator. It was common knowledge that he would cut and thresh that first load green if he had to, take a poor grade from Max Harrison's elevator for it, rather than have one of his neighbors carry off the honors. Each year he would be in a day or two sooner because he had heard that someone was "going to pull a fast one" and beat him for once. Then, after maintaining the legend, faithfully documented by the Lobb girls in *The Missenden Thunderbolt,* he would relax for two or three weeks — a month if necessary — while the rest of his grain ripened before finishing his harvesting.

No one called Jack Smythe a character although he was one, and an individualist too. Certain of the good people of Minby said he had an awful seamy side about him. I was in the dark about what this implied as a kid, although I suspected all kinds of amazing things. . . . The so-called "seamy" things I did hear only added to the tremendous charm he held for me. Certainly the juiciest tidbits Angèle related to Mom concerned Old Jack.

Old Jack was over fifty at the turn of the century and had seen service in the South African war. He was virile enough, had black enough hair, and was a skillful enough liar to enlist in the Canadian Expeditionary Forces in 1914 and to see that war through to the end.

George Milford, one of his old army buddies, used to say a bit maliciously that the only shells Old Jack Smythe heard bursting around him in France were the eggshells he himself was cracking in the field kitchen.

In 1928 Old Jack was eighty, give or take a year or two, looked sixty, and in spite of a heavy shock of hair that was now pure white, he was as active in *every* respect as a man of forty. Certainly the most interesting rumors concerning him confirmed this last remark. Married three times, he had children from three to sixty-three, and grandchildren and great-grandchildren in every Province of Canada and in the northern States.

Now why should Old Jack take a fancy to me? Was he responding unbeknownst to the tremendous feeling of attraction he had for me? Perhaps. I idolized him, he couldn't have helped knowing it. If he was driving his big Reo truck into or out of town, and if he passed me on the road and recognized me, he would immediately pull over with his truck and take me along — even if he had been traveling at thirty-five or forty miles an hour. Once or twice when he was going *out* of town he told me to hop in beside him and he'd drive me back. Yet he would make his own kids *walk* into town to pick up something he had absentmindedly forgotten.

Old Jack was in a way a hail fellow well met everywhere but at home; there he was a belligerent and despotic old tyrant. He admired my Dad tremendously — Dad was young enough to have been his son — and perhaps his esteem for him just bubbled over to the second generation to me. That didn't mean he liked *all* Swedes, however — he loathed "Uncle" Martin, Dad's Old Country friend, and the first question he would invariably ask me when I hopped up in the cab beside him was: "What's that crooked son-of-a-bitch of a Martin Eriksson up to now?"

Once or twice the odd remark escaped him which led me to believe that he abhorred Mrs. Red Blaine even more than he detested "Uncle" Martin. This was quite true, a fact which was to be confirmed in a most surprising manner some months later on. Mrs. Blaine had a wicked tongue and she had once made the mistake of saying some very uncomplimentary things about Mr. Smythe. Old Jack wasn't the sort of person to let such remarks go unanswered but he had different tactics when dealing with a woman.

Old Jack was Irish. He sang his songs and recited his own execrable poetry, chiefly ballads, which he had composed about cowboy life, or his adventures in the bush country. The cowboy stuff was terrible because it was only a rehash of other cowboy songs he had heard. Since Old Jack didn't always understand what *he* heard, and since I, when I listened to his vocalizing didn't understand much of what *I* heard, confusion was invariably the result. A part of one of his songs went as follows:

"Beat the drum slowly,
Play the vi', Foley!"

That was my first interpretation of those two lines; I assumed that if the word "saxophone" could be abbreviated to "sax," so, too, could "violin" be abbreviated to "vi"; Jack's hired man, another Irishman like himself, was Tim Foley. When I repeated this line at home, Dad remarked with an amused smile, that it was probably something else. Sure enough, when I heard the song again some time later, it wasn't the Irishman Foley who was playing but some Swede:

"Beat the drum slowly,
Play the fife, Oley!"

When Jack sang that song first, I was sure it was about a cowboy, an Indian cowboy by the name of Ny-Ma-Dyne, because it always ended up,

"Ny-Ma-Dyne cowboy
N'I know I done wrong."
It seems to me there was another line in the song somewhere that went,
"God shot me through the heart,
Ny-Ma-Dyne today!"
but that must have been wrong too. No good Catholic
would accuse his Lord of breaking one of his own com-
mandments, and the sixth one at that.

Old Jack's bush-country material, on the other hand,
had an authentic ring to it, since he usually related his
own experiences up North. He had to know his songs
by heart because the only words he could draw (he could-
n't write) were his first and about half of his last name.
Mrs. Red Blaine kept him off the Minby Community
Hall Board once by saying the board members should
at least be able to read and write. That, as a matter
of fact, was what Old Jack held against her, that was
the score he dreamed one day of settling with her.

Jack, since he couldn't read, naturally depended on
his memory. So any new words he heard, or anything
more than three syllables, often underwent radical
changes from the time it entered his ears and left again
via his mouth.

For a good while Old Jack was a convinced British
Israelite and the fantastic conception he imparted of this
to others in his mixed-up missionary zeal, was extremely
original to say the least. His enthusiasm did other things
to his mispronunciation. He had the merit, however, of
being consistent in his deformation of the English language which would almost make one believe that the
systematically badly pronounced words followed definite
sound shifts. The word "municipality" invariably came
out "municispelicy"; when he talked about Lionel
Stephenson's "ninvention" which he most often and
most enthusiastically did (was he, perchance, one of Mr.

Stephenson's secret backers?) it was to say, among other things, that it would "revelize" the world because Lionel had finally harnessed "perennial" motion.

Added to the above monstrosities was the consistent insertion of an "e" or often of an "ie" after certain consonants when he formed the plural. One "post" in the plural became two "postes," one "desk," two "deskes," etc., and when the plural of "horse" became "horsies" one thought for a moment that this white-haired despotic old tyrant was lapsing into baby talk, or talking to one of his grandchildren. Often when he spoke, a final "g" was pronounced "k," "nothing" and "something" becoming "nothink" and somethink" respectively.

Once this year Thornton in his special train stopped in Missenden for a few hours to "come into contact with the people out West." Old Jack said that Sir Thornton might just as well have stayed at home back East, he couldn't see "nothink" from the back of his special car.

"If he'd of got out and let me *chiffonier* him around, I'd a showed him a think or two!"

Along with Jack's first load of grain each year, a claim he was to maintain for many years, was another tradition. This was the two tremendous "feeds" he put on annually. They were known far and wide, miles beyond what could be considered Minby territory. Until Dad took us all to the States one year to visit our Uncle Hasse when I saw entire fields of corn for the first time, I thought that Old Jack was the only man in the wide wide world who grew more than two rows of it since that was about all anybody else in Minby had.

Jack had acres of corn, and each fall, three nights hand running, he would boil the sweetest of cobs for his guests. There were quart sealers of butter, too, into which the freshly boiled cob could be plunged. Whole families drove incredibly long distances to participate, some coming every night for the three nights. As time

went on, more and more of the travelers staying at Müller's Hotel got to hear about it and they would time
their trip so as to include Jack's corn feed in that week's
itinerary. The Müllers didn't mind the competition — on
the contrary! Although they charged the unheard of price
of *fifty cents* for their meals, they claimed they made
nothing on them anyway. Either Mr. or Mrs Müller generally went out to Smythes' too, the other one staying at
home to run the hotel. Jack's feed was, in effect, a huge
municipal picnic, since most of the "municispelicy" was
there.

Why did Mr. Smythe have his feed each year? Was
it just his exuberant natural generosity, the irrepressible
impulse or compulsion to do something in the grand
manner? It would have been hard to find an ulterior
motive. When the third and last evening was over, the
people picked and took home as much of the remaining
corn as they liked. When asked why he went to all the
trouble, his reply was always the same: "Hell, it don't
cost nothink." His numerous family, from his browbeaten nervous mouse of a wife right down to those of
his kids old enough to assist, he ordered around like
lackeys at these functions.

The second "feed," which was also held in the fall,
was much more esoteric in character; it was held one
evening only and was exclusively for men. Jack not only
slaughtered the English language, but he did all the slaugh-
tering for the Minby Beef Ring as well. It was thus easy
for him to gather together the ingredients for his annual
tripe feed. He also had lamb fries for anyone curious
enough to try them, and when I asked Mom what *that*
was, she said it "isn't good to know . . ." I, of course,
was too young to attend this second feed; and since my
father never drank liquor of any kind, he only put in
token appearances. Since practically every other male
in the district — the most Fundamental Minby Bethelites

excepted, of course — *did* drink and *did* attend, it was common knowledge what went on at this second pow-wow. The Bethel Fundamentalists went further afield when they wanted tripe . . .

"Uncle" Martin who had closed up his office once years back when he had rheumatism so bad he thought he was going to die, made a near miraculous recovery when he recalled that Jack's tripe feed was being held that evening . . .

When Reverend Kreuz, our new minister, heard about Old Jack's yearly gathering, his first eager, interested queries were of a distinctly approving nature . . .

"And do so many people like tripe around Minby?"

Angèle, who shared my Dad's antipathy for strong drink, piped up acidly, "After they've been there a half an hour it don' matter if they don' like tripe, they don' know what they're eating anyway!"

I, alas, was never old enough to attend one of these Lucullian repasts "for men only." But then could what went on have been more ribald, more hair-raising than some of Old Jack's other adventures which he related to me?

Now why, precisely, did I like this old sinner? True, Old Jack was in the "mustn't touch" category and that had a devastating charm all of its own. He was a bit of a Wild West hero too. I would somehow put him in the same big bag of associations as Kit Carson and Tom Mix; I later added Mark Twain, because Old Jack looked amazingly like him, though on a more robust scale. For all of me Old Jack and the last three named could have been contemporaries. And then when I heard about Sohrab and Rustum in school, I felt Rustum would have had to be Old Jack's double, except that the Minby Rustum didn't have a son equal to Sohrab.

I never once saw Old Jack on a horse, but he always wore a Stetson at a racy angle. He was, in spite of his age, perhaps because of his age, the most magnificent male specimen around Minby. Some of the rumors that floated back to our village from the city when he had been down for a long weekend or from Calgary when he had been to the Stampede, positively left one dreamy-eyed. There just seemed to be something magnificent about this Old Sire that had so successfully stood the test and the rigors of time. He was conscious of his worth as a man — he didn't "take *nothink* from nobody." He was seen on more than one occasion, fists up, in front of Barney Grant's Pool Room ready to prove it — the other always backed down. Taking him on would have been like walking into a windmill.

Old Jack really enjoyed life to the full. That was obvious whenever I saw him, and just as obvious from the questions he'd ask me when I jumped up in his cab beside him. And it made me feel so big and important when he'd take me into his somewhat off-color confidences.

It was within a month after Reverend Kreuz's arrival, in one of our Saturday School classes, that I learned from our minister what a horrible and pestiferous creature a Roman Catholic was. Since Old Jack was nominally one of these — certainly a non-practicing one — it shook me, leaving my admiration of him somewhat open to question. But not for very long. Reverend Kreuz might be right in *some* of his pronouncements, but when it came to *my good friend* Mr. Smythe, I'd make up my mind myself.

THE CALDWELLS

IT WAS a treat to drive with my Dad "out in the country" as he called it; but the chances of such a trip dwindled to zero after Reverend Kreuz's arrival — he had, so to speak, taken over. My brother Kalle generally got to go. My Saturday morning was now monopolized by Saturday School. It seemed, at first, until I got settled into a routine, that if I hadn't catechism to prepare for that, then I had hymns to practice for church next day.

This was only early October. Christmas was still well over two months away, yet we were already learning special hymns and recitations for it. In short the youngsters belonging to our long-dormant congregation had suddenly become very religion-minded. When Dad told me this day to hop into the "bug" with him, I didn't even ask where we were going. We would be leaving Minby for an hour or two. Wasn't that enough?

We weren't more than a mile out of town when the cut-down Model T began to misperform. Instead of continuing west, Dad took a quick swing over by our own farm which was only a half mile south, driving the "bug" up alongside our Fordson tractor. Then followed a little lesson in elementary Model T Ford mechanics, a lesson I had already seen Dad give my older brother Kalle.

Leaving the gas lever up where the motor was unlikely to start, and turning the key from "Mag" (magneto) over to "Bat" (battery), Dad went around to the front of the "bug" and slowly turned the engine over. My job was to see which one of the four coils wasn't buzzing properly.

Dad wasn't in a hurry that day; he could have found out alone by trial and error what ailed the little flivver but he wanted to give me the feeling I was helping. Dad was always giving us little lessons. For him no knowledge was useless, however unrelated to the thing in hand — you could never tell when it would "come in handy" he would say or, more often, "It doesn't cost anything to carry 'round."

When I decided which one of the coils wasn't functioning properly — I could see the blue-white sparks from the top of the good coils and hear them buzzing like oversize infuriated mosquitoes — Dad came back to the car, bringing with him a new coil from the Fordson. This he quickly exchanged with the weak one from the coil box in the car. Then, pulling down the gas lever once more, he gave a heave on the crank, and the Model T shook into life on all four; there was just a split second's hesitation when he turned the key from "Bat" back to "Mag" — it was a different car.

My Dad had long ago explained to Kalle and me how the magneto worked, why it would give a stronger spark than the battery, and why at nights the lights got stronger the faster we drove. With brand-new, tight-fitting transmission linings in the "bug," the little converted Ford was impatient to move on. For the second time we were off.

Leaving the farm we retraced the half mile north until we were back on the east-west road which would take us out to Caldwells. The "bug" really purred along now. We only met a few cars, one of which — another Model T — belonged to the Rawleigh man. He waved to us, and we to him — it was as if the cars they drove made the two owners members of the same fraternity.

We met still fewer teams coming to town, since it was well on into the noon hour. We were therefore very surprised to meet Friedrich Schaller on his way in, since he lived about as far out as anyone who dealt in Minby. Didn't he have at least three more miles to go to reach town? In just a few hours he should be heading back home again!

Whenever I saw Mr. Schaller I always thought of the *schwarzer Geiger,* the "dark fiddler" in the story Mom's friend Mrs. Milford used to tell us. He looked blacker and grimmer than I had ever seen him, and if he could play a violin at all, which was doubtful, he wouldn't have been in any mood to play that day. Dad explained to me that Mr. Schaller hadn't got over the loss of his little boy. His son had died rather tragically just a short while back trying to get out of the grain box. To make matters worse, his wife had blamed the accident on him for not taking the boy along with him to the field that day. Now she had left, taking their two little girls with her to her home in the States. Mr. Schaller was alone on the farm once more managing as best he could, just as he had done before they were married. Dad gave him plenty of berth as we passed, but Mr. Schaller looked morosely ahead of him, and didn't even acknowledge my father's friendly greeting. Perhaps he didn't see him.

We followed "Young Jack" Smythe at a snail's pace for a quarter of a mile before we were finally able to pass. Old Jack, his Dad, part-time well digger, butcher for the beef ring, cultivator of corn *par excellence,* also owned a magnificent Clydesdale stallion. Young Jack was a familiar sight on the country roads as he took the stallion around to make his calls. The sorry-looking mare pulling the two-wheel cart in which Young Jack sat, was in startling contrast to the big imposing stud which was tied short and following behind. The mare and cart kept to the right of the road where they belonged, but the stallion bringing up the rear tacked as it followed, effectively blocking the whole left half of the road where we wanted to go by.

Schaller's melancholy countenance must have been contagious because Mr. Caldwell was in just as pessimistic a mood when we drove into his yard. Dad headed straight for the machine shed, hopped out of the "bug," his tool box in one hand, with me trailing along after him.

It was immediately clear to my father that this farmer was once more having domestic troubles and that he had only called to get things off his mind. He didn't want any repair work done — that had been his pretext to get Dad to drive out.

It wasn't the first time Mr. Caldwell had called upon my father in this way; although Dad wasn't too surprised that he had made the long trip out for nothing he was obviously more than a bit vexed, for when he had an hour to spare, which wasn't often, he had countless things of his own to do. I kept my distance and pretended to be busy with something else. Even if I didn't catch *all* of what was said — it wasn't meant for my ears anyway — I heard more than enough to know what it was all about.

Frank Caldwell was a man of about sixty, fifteen or twenty years older than my father; his wife was perhaps five years younger than he. It was a secret to no one in Minby that when he met Mrs. Caldwell at the train fifteen years before it was the culminating point of a Home Loving Hearts Romance. They were married within the week and before the year was out their only daughter was born. It was generally acknowledged too, in view of Mrs. Caldwell's age, that had the girl not arrived when she did, she wouldn't have arrived at all.

Mrs. Caldwell quickly became the backbone of her church, the First Presbyterian, which was across the way from our house. Soon the most influential member of the congregation, nothing was planned or carried out without her approval. Angèle told Mom once that the quickest way for anyone in that congregation to get anything done was to put the words into Mrs. Caldwell's mouth and make her think the idea was hers.

Already in her first year in Minby Mrs. Caldwell had organized an outdoor service in *her* grove near *her* home, and it became an event which was held every year thereafter. Like Jack Smythe's two annual feeds, this outdoor service was soon an established Minby tradition, although one didn't mention such radically different events (or persons) in the same breath.

Before the arrival of Reverend Kreuz, and in the absence of a pastor for our church, my parents sporadically attended the other Protestant churches; but our whole family had driven out to the Caldwell outdoor services every year. I know I enjoyed watching the ball game or participating in the picnic which preceded the evening activities, but I would have been happier if we had gone home *before* her evening service instead of after. "Worshipping in the Grove" was evidently the price Dad expected us to pay for the "goodies" we had had in the afternoon although he would never have put it that way.

Twice a week, for years now, winter and summer alike, I had seen Mr. and Mrs. Caldwell and their daughter come into town. They came in first on Saturday afternoon when the girl was brought to our place to Mrs. Tischler for her music lesson; and they would drive the long way in again the very next day to attend the Presbyterian service. Outwardly, one would have thought it was a tightly knit little family that moves as one person, with Unity and Harmony as its *Leitmotiv*.

"... and I haven't slept with her since before the kid was born, Ingve, she just moved my stuff out of the clothes closet the day she knew she was pregnant and I've never seen the inside of that bedroom since . . ."

I didn't hear all the exchange between my Dad and Mr. Caldwell; but a few facts were certain, "it has gone on too many years," "I have been made a fool of," "I have been a fool to turn the farm over to her," "I am my wife's own lackey" but "I'll get even with her, I'll . . . I'll . . .." but at this point he would throw up his hands, contradicting himself since he didn't know what he could do.

That's all he had wanted to discuss with my father. Dad vaguely hemmed and hawed, cleared his throat several times as he generally did before saying anything, but his only remark was that it was really none of his business. Didn't Mr. Caldwell know my Dad well enough *not* to ask his advice? Especially in a matter of so personal a nature?

"Have you discussed it with your minister?" asked Dad finally, trying to be helpful.

"The minister?" snorted Mr. Caldwell in a jeering, scornful tone of voice.

All Mr. Caldwell could think of now was getting even. And it reminded me of Old Jack Smythe figuring out a way to settle his score with Mrs. Red Blaine.

"I've thought of pulling out, Ingve, but at my age . . . This is hell, I can tell you. The kid doesn't even talk to me. Thank God she looks like her mother — I hope to Christ she's *all* hers . . . I'll get even, by Jesus, just you wait and see if I don't, *just see if I don't!* She'll pay me for every cent she's taken, interest and principal; she'll pay me for every humiliation she's given me, interest and principal too, by Christ . . ."

We didn't stay much longer. Dad was flushed in the face, embarrassed, impatient to get away — he didn't enjoy this spectacle at all. He was extremely thoughtful all the way home, no doubt wondering, as I was, what deviltry Mr. Caldwell was up to and how he was going to "make her pay."

We had stayed well past dinner time yet Mrs. Caldwell hadn't invited us in to eat. Now I began to understand why. Many times in the past I had been out with my Dad to other farms, and at meal time the farmer's wife always offered "pot luck." Wasn't that part of the fun of making the trip with my Dad? These women seemed to like nothing better than to have a visitor stay for a meal with a bit of first-hand news from Minby.

I wondered afterwards, mulling over in my mind what I had overheard that day between Mr. Caldwell and my Dad, if the husband and wife even ate at the same table. Why should they have, if they didn't sleep together and if they didn't speak to one another? If she treated him like a dog as Mr. Caldwell twice said, did she just set out a tin plate for him on the back steps . . .?

That little trip gave me a lot to think about. I was still naive enough to think that most husbands and wives got along like my own Dad and Mom. So I watched Mr. and Mrs. Caldwell thereafter getting out of the car when they came to town. If they presented from a distance the outward signs of a happy little family, dressed in their Sunday best as they arrived for their weekly religious service, he hypocritically hurrying around to her side of the car to open the door and help her out, she hypocritically allowing him to perform these obsequious services for her, it was obvious that the only words exchanged were between mother and daughter.

TRUTH AND POETRY

THE Minby fowl suppers were always followed by a concert. This one Friday evening, November 23, 1928, was no exception. I had hoped to hear Barney Grant sing "Felix the Cat," or Grandpa Barnett do one of his readings. But I was doomed to disappointment this night.

The newest Saints on the Bethel Calendar were unfamiliar to me. Mrs. Bennett, treasurer of the Bethel Ladies Aid, had learned that Albert Whitmore, the most recent addition to their congregation, could sing. He was the new bank clerk who had come in the fall and who had stayed on to run the Searle elevator after the bank closed. His mother could sing too, and they had *offered* their services tonight. Angèle, our hired girl, said afterwards, that when anyone offers to sing, in a small town the size of Minby, before ascertaining if there isn't someone there who *can,* then "you badder watch out!"

It turned out that Mrs. Whitmore and her son Albert, plus another Bennett "surprise," entertained us that evening. When "Whispering Hope" was announced as the first number I suspected that the rest of the Whitmore offerings would fit the same doleful pattern.

For me, ten years old at the time, Mrs. Whitmore was really ancient, at least *fifty* anyway, and prim — that was the word Angèle used — like the two old-maid Lobb sisters. She wore low-heeled shoes, looked severely ahead of her and never once moved her head or eyes while she sang; and her son, whom the gang in the Pool Room called "Bertie" or just "Momma's boy" after this night, picked out some spot in the upper right-hand corner of the hall from which he never removed his gaze.

Mrs. Dahlke who was playing the accompaniment, and who had always played an organ, was trying to pump the hall piano in the same manner as she pumped her organ back on the farm. She had been captivated by Mrs. Whitmore. Mrs. Whitmore wore a hat with a veil, so Mrs. Dahlke decided she should put a veil on hers too. She therefore hung a rather heavy one, one about six inches wide, on her old hat, the same old hat we had seen her wear on all occasions. It hung down thick and black like a heavy little curtain, swaying back and forth in front of her face as she herself swayed in front of the piano. It proved such an obstacle to her note reading that she took it off with an apologetic smile to the audience after the first number. It is true that her playing improved tremendously but it was still bad.

Old Jack Smythe, whose reputation as a singer wasn't based on the type of song Bertie and his Mommie had in their repertoire, nevertheless knew the "Church in the Wildwood" which the Whitmores offered as their closing number. When mother and son intoned the last chorus, inviting us all to come to the church in the wildwood, Old Jack chimed in first of all with a low whistle, and finally with a "Come, come, come" in a bass which the two on the stage could not hear, but which was perfectly audible to the rest of the audience. It looked for all the world as if he was singing to Mrs. Whitmore. The volunteer singers wondered no doubt why they had touched the Minby audience with that particular song and not the others, since the applause this time, instead of being politely restrained, was deafening.

Mrs. Bennett's second surprise that evening was her very own niece who had once lived in Minby. I had seen this niece several times in the past when she was up from the city; but didn't know she was a musician. And she had surely changed! One of her big front teeth overlapped the other making her look like Peter Rabbit.

She was scrawny and she wore the highest-heeled shoes ever seen in our town, and she came hurrying out with fast little steps to the stage, talking as she came. What vivacity! She teetered to a stop, music in one hand, adjusting her curly hair for the last time with the other.

Miss Bennett wasn't just going to play for us, she gushed, taking up her position more or less in the center of the stage, instead she was going to give us a Master Lesson. The piece she had chosen was "In a Persian Market." She gave some biographical detail about the composer, where he lived, what else he had written; then hurrying out to the very edge of the platform, a big smile on her face, she beamed down to ask "if any of the kiddies" had heard about Persia or knew what a market was.

Two little "kiddies" had their hands up instantly, but both were wrong. The first little girl thought it might be Carwardines' farm, because wasn't that where she had got her Persian cat? The other thought it was Doyles' farm, another mile down the road, the only farm in Minby boasting sheep, and she thought that Doyles' sheep and Persian lambs might be the same. By the time Miss Bennett got this straightened out, she had completely run out of small talk, and she hadn't as much to say about Persia and market places as she had thought; it was now time for the Mistress of the Keyboard to massacre the masterpiece itself.

Crystal Bennett could *not* play. Had she had any idea about music at all she would have surely selected some other piece. She hustled over to the piano on her spindly heels, explaining once more over her shoulder to the kiddies what a market was, telling us all to pretend we were there while she performed.

As Crystal played, she came to full stops to declaim aloud details and instructions which the author had put in, plus a multitude of others that he had never dreamed of. Her scrawny elbows flew out in all directions during her rendition. If there was little one could say for her interpretation, one could at least say it was loud, and "Scotty" Evans behind me was audibly wondering "where does such a tiny thing get so much *stranth* to play like that!"

If there were parts that Crystal liked — and indeed there were some sections she liked *very* much — she played them over and over again, compensating, no doubt, for the more difficult parts which she omitted. She came to a full stop each time to tell us kiddies when the temple bell was ringing and ask us if we liked it. When we hollered and screamed "yass, yass," she made the temple bell ring three or four times more, bringing the surprised Persians down to their knees and Mecca-wards again. Then really bending down over the ivories, her nose at times just inches away from the keys as she strove for effects, she banged the temple bells again in a crashing *grande finale*.

The Minby Community Hall piano was never the same afterwards. Such thunderous applause, and such stamping of feet had seldom been heard in our town. Miss Bennett promised to come back next year and do "In a Monastery Garden" by the same composer.

Miss Lobb, Minby's correspondent for the weekly *Missenden Thunderbolt,* could be seen after the program, notebook in hand, obtaining other bits of information from the guest star about her performance that evening. Under the pen of a poet, truth gives way to sheer poetry. This is what appeared in *The Missenden Thunderbolt* the following week.

Minby

The Bethel Tabernacle Annual Fowl Supper and Concert was held in the Minby Community Hall with a goodly crowd in attendance. Again the Bethel Ladies Aid showed how equal they were to the task of looking after the inner man, providing tempting viands in bountiful quantities under which the heaping tables fairly groaned.

The concert opened with Reverend Galway from Missenden as guest speaker for the evening. He chose as his theme the title of the well-known hymn "O Come, Everyone that Thirsteth." By sheer coincidence this number was included among the delightful selections so generously offered by Mrs. Whitmore and her son Albert, all of which were warmly received.

Would that a muse of fire were mine to command in praise of our own Crystal Bennett, the glory of our own little Minby, who was in town on a short visit. Not because Crystal is so youthful and happy in her work, but because she is making music at a level that is very high by anyone's standards. Of all the works on the Fowl Supper to date in Minby, the most involving was surely her selection. This cannot possibly be grasped at a first hearing, creating at once both fascination and desire for further acquaintance. It has what every fine work of art strives for: at once a formal balance and perspective and a lively sense of the present. The kiddies in the audience were enthralled — this will be a memorable experience for all of them. Listening to this music, one knows that music is indivisible — that serialism, the sonorities of the piano are one for a composer and for an interpreter (such as our Crystal!) whose vision can perceive and encompass them all.

This young musician from whom we received so much is *ours*. And we can be justly proud of her. Our own Crystal is not, or should not be merely a source of reflected glory, but rather she should become a torch to set fire to the musical community in the country as a whole. Do come again next year, Crystal! Welcome back!

Christina Lobb, your Minby correspondent.

MINBY MYSTERIES

WE had only been back in school a few minutes when a knock came at the door. Could it be the inspector? Mr. Mitchell returned, bringing a stranger back into the classroom with him.

He was an inspector, but not the school inspector. He had been checking the rails, telephone poles and telephone lines along the track; now he was saying that the kids in Minby were the most destructive he had seen. There were more broken insulators on the poles between Culbertson and Minby than he had seen anywhere until he had come to the stretch between Minby and Missenden which was worse! Didn't we know better than to throw rocks at them? Didn't we know better than cleaning them off with a twenty-two? Couldn't he see where the spent lead had gone into the stringers? That was sheer vandalism and he was going to report us to the police.

We all looked stupidly from one to another. Who *had* done it?

Who hadn't at some time or other thrown a rock at an insulator? But there weren't many boys at school with a twenty-two. Nor was there any point in wasting shells on insulators when you could get three cents a tail shooting gophers. And shooting at a live target was much more fun. Who would walk all the way down to Culbertson just to break insulators?

At three o'clock our room paraded down to the loading platform by the tracks where the Tree Planting Car had been dropped off the night before. The Government was sending it around again to the different prairie points in an attempt to stimulate farmers to plant more trees. The Junior Room had been down just before us to see the movies. Now it was our turn.

We found the portion of the program devoted to tree planting dull. We found the film with Andy Gump sleepwalking very interesting. Before we left, however, the man told us he had a visitor who wanted to have a word with us. It was the man with his harangue about the insulators again. In the whole province he hadn't seen so many broken ones until he came to Minby. Why he . . .

That same evening the Wheat Pool put on a free picture show in the Community Hall. First we saw a comic feature starring Harold Lloyd, then a couple of twenty-minute Charlie Chaplin shorts, then there was a concert when the movie operator's daughter got up on stage and did some wonderful tap dancing for us. For a special Spanish number, she wore a dark red dress with a long train, and lots of white frills. She threw her legs so high in the air at times that we saw she was wearing red and white panties to match.

The show over, the people began getting up from their seats. A few of the men started to clear the benches out of the way for the dance when the Wheat Pool man announced that there was a gentleman in the audience who wanted to have a word.

It was the "insulator" man again. I knew some of the sentences by heart now. He glared at the adults in the audience as he ranted, concluding that it was as much their fault as the kids'.

There was a final echo at our place, for next morning at the breakfast table, Dad faced us grimly, his knife in one hand, his fork in the other, both fists on the table. He still hadn't started to eat. He must have thought that the telephone inspector's tirade had been directed at *him* last night, and that it was *his* kids, the Viggos, who had committed the vandalism.

"If I ever hear of you throwing stones at insulators," Dad said ominously, "You'll sure catch it. You'll get the worst trashing . . ."

Dad didn't bawl us out about the *other* matter: it would have embarrassed him to even mention it. Before midnight, the Wheat Pool man had interrupted the dance long enough to make an announcement:

"Will the souvenir hunter who took my daughter's panties from the dressing room kindly return them. She'll need them tomorrow night in Culbertson."

We never found out who the insulator-breaking fanatic was. But that incident, together with what happened at the Wheat Pool program set Mom and Angèle to whispering about Minby's most picturesque mystery of all! Angèle and several other girls at least *once,* and Mrs. Barry on *several* occasions, had had their panties stolen off the line when they had been left out overnight. Of course it had to be someone they knew, someone they probably were seeing every day. It was certainly the same person last night, "up to his tricks" once more.

Of course . . . But who?

HAIRCUT

FOR three or four weeks, since the middle of November, placards had been posted all over Minby telling us that the Jubilee Entertainers were coming. Kalle and I had both saved up enough so we could hear them. Before we could go, however, we would have to go to Mr. Grant's for a haircut. Dad had now been gone five days. In the rush of packing and final preparations for the trip to Sweden he hadn't had time to give us our usual trim.

I had passed by the Pool Room and Barber Shop practically every day since I was old enough to walk. It was on Main Street between the old claptrap of a hotel and Stewart's store, so it was impossible to go downtown and miss it. Very seldom did I venture in, however. The Pool Room was in the forbidden fruit category. Dad told us more than once that kids had no business in there.

Mr. Grant, the proprietor, was an extraordinary individual for Minby; but no matter what his original plans were for operating a business of this kind, he had to conform to the pattern and standards set by his predecessors. Did he really expect to maintain the atmosphere of a dignified English Billiard Club Room, or a Gentleman's Barber Shop in Minby? Mr. Grant had to reckon with his clientele — he would have gone bankrupt the first month if he hadn't.

The Pool Room and Barber Shop, long before Mr. Grant's arrival in Minby, had been the favorite congregating place of the rummy players, the dirty-storytellers, the men from the track when their work was done or when they were out of work, and on top of it all, for the village loungers, be they reckoned as Minby bums or not. Dad, no doubt, tarred all the habitués with the same stick. If each didn't shoot a game of snooker every day, or if each of them didn't get his hair trimmed every two or three weeks, it was nevertheless their periodic games, their occasional haircuts collectively that kept Mr. Grant in business.

More than once I heard Angèle tell Mom that she would prefer to go up the dirt road *behind* the Pool Hall rather than use the board sidewalk in front. There was always that gang of men, she said, and they always stared at her when she walked past as if she didn't have a stitch on; and as soon as she *was* past, and not even out of earshot, she could hear them speculating about her and Gene, and asking one another if there would "be anything new besides the wedding cake when they get married . . ." or "if they'll find it any different with their boots off . . ."

Haircuts were most often done all day Saturday, starting early in the morning; they were also done the late afternoons and evenings on those days when a dance or concert was held; otherwise the establishment could often be as quiet as a tomb during the day.

It wasn't unusual to see three or four of the local farmers at a dance with red sunburned necks that turned abruptly white for an inch and a half, as if their collar had suddenly shifted upwards because Barney Grant had cut away a thick layer of protective hair only an hour or so before. My dad thought that two to three weeks between trims was long enough; some of Barney's customers who believed in getting their money's worth waited two or three months.

Mr. Grant was the last man one would expect to find operating a Pool Room in a small town like Minby. He was a real gentleman, more so even than "Gentleman" Max Harrison, the elevator man. On Sundays with his pinstripe black suit and gray Homberg hat, and his gold-capped front tooth flashing in the sun, he could

have been mistaken for one of the bank managers —
that is while the Dominion and the Standard banks were
still open.

When there were no customers to be served, Mr.
Grant liked nothing better than to close the front door
and sing. He didn't have the sort of amateur voice one
would expect to hear in an out-of-the-way place like
Minby either, but a real professionally trained singer's
voice.

Mr. Grant had been in Minby several years and had
married Miss Fraser, my second teacher. Although I
heard him sing once or twice a year at the Fowl Suppers
and other concerts, beyond saying "hello" to him once
or twice I had never really spoken to him. Yet he was
my friend. I was walking past his place one day when
one of the bums, one of the dumb Franklins, hollered
"Hello Froggy" at me because I was wearing glasses.
Erik Haugen was with me and laughed — he thought
that was a big joke and called me "Froggy" too.

"O.K. wise guys," said Mr. Grant at the time, "I
wear glasses too. Now which one of you would like to
call *me* Froggy?"

What did Mr. Grant begin to talk about when he
started to cut my hair? They say a good barber is conver-
sant on *all* subjects. It wasn't long, in any event, before
I had swung the conversation to music.

"Do you know lots more pieces like 'Felix'?"

"Felix" was my favorite of all my favorites . . .

"Felix? . . . Where did you ever hear of Felix?"
asked Mr. Grant innocently, never missing a snip with
his scissors. Had it not been for him, no one in Minby
would have heard of Felix and how he "kep' on walkin'
still . . ."

Mr. Grant laughed with amusement as I recited what
I remembered of the lyrics. Maybe I did get them somewhat garbled, but the content was there and the rhyme

right; I added or improvised a few lines that weren't quite like the original. When I recalled how "by the train from Dover" Felix "had his tail run over" it was too much for him; I could see him in the mirror, clearing his throat, his eyes sparkling . . . With his scissors in one hand, and the comb in the other, he took up the chorus from there to the end, singing out how Felix "wagged his nothin' in the air and kep' on walkin' still."

Was it my imagination playing tricks on me? The big mirror that was fully three feet wide and four feet high and solidly attached to the wall trembled . . . The bottles of hair lotion, aftershave water and brilliantine danced on the shelves from his powerful voice and I could feel the chair quiver from the vibration of his chest and stomach as he pressed into the back for support as his voice swelled in the *crescendo*. I had goose pimples all over!

Both of us laughed over the song; then he laughed louder still afterwards, all by himself.
"Sing 'Freshie'!" I asked.
" 'Freshie'? Never heard of it."
"Sure, you know it, it's got that funny part in it!"
"What funny part? How does it go?"
I didn't know exactly either, but there were some lines like,
"Why do they all pick on Freshie?
He's a nut,
Nothing but,
The squirrels all hang around him."
But Mr. Grant swore he didn't know it. I could see in the mirror that he meant it and that really puzzled me: If I hadn't learned it from Mr. Grant, then where else could I have picked it up? It wasn't one of our records at home — they were too old for that.
"Well, then, how about 'Barney Google'?" I asked.

"Ah," said Mr. Grant with mock disgust, "you don't want to hear that!"

There was nothing I wanted to hear more at that moment than those lines "Barney Google, with them goo- goo- googley eyes, Barney Google, with a wife three times his size . . ."

I regretted there wasn't a piano to accompany him and I said so.

"You play the piano, don't you Wally?"

I was flattered to hear that he not only knew that I played the piano but that of the four Viggo boys I was Wally. Indeed it made me comfortably warm all over to hear this adult addressing me by my first name. So many times when I was asked my name I'd say "Viggo," and when they'd next ask "Kalle"? I'd always have to explain that I was the *other* one, the *next* one . . .

"You'll have to come down to our place some time, Wally. Mrs. Grant and I are getting a new piano, a brand new player piano."

"A player piano? Aren't *all* pianos players?"

"A player piano is something different, it's one you don't have to play, it's one that plays all by itself."

If I hadn't been watching Mr. Grant's reflection in the mirror, I would have thought he was pulling my leg. After all that was a little strong, a piano that played by itself . . .

"But who presses the keys . . . How does it know . . . How . . .?"

"You just put a roll into it, a music roll, a special one for each piece, and then pump with your feet like an organ to get it going. The music comes out all by itself after that."

That was simply too much for me to grasp. He had to tell me all over again. I was baptized Waldemar Edvard Viggo, but my middle name should have been "skeptical" instead. I would simply have to see this before I would believe. Or check with Dad when he got home from Sweden.

These doubts were still chasing one another around in my head when Mr. Grant splashed what was left of my hair with his smelliest, oiliest hair tonic; it was almost ice cold from standing on the shelf next to the wall. It was probably some preparation exclusively for kids, for no self-respecting adult male would have allowed himself to go around smelling like a bordello.

"That's Siberian Bear Oil, Wally." A few seconds' pause, "Yes, Wally, genuine Siberian Bear Oil — my very last bottle!"

A quick glance into his mirror for verification and I could see of course that Mr. Grant was dead serious . . .

"Is it like the radio at all?"

"The Siberian Bear Oil?"

"No, the player piano you were talking about, the one you're going to get."

"It looks exactly like any other piano. You can play it too, like an ordinary piano afterwards, when you take the roll out. I'm not fooling you Wally, I'll be sure to ask you down some time to hear it. And if I don't ask you, you remind me, eh?"

Would I remind him!

Mr. Grant held a smaller mirror with both hands behind my head and I glanced into the big mirror in front of me, critically examining my haircut, I, who was seeing the back of my head for the first time in my life. Then I slid off the big chair on to the floor. I was finished.

Not until I got home and Mom asked me how much a boy's haircut was did I realize that neither I nor Mr. Grant had remembered that I hadn't paid.

What better excuse to go down and see him again?

THE LESSONS

THE FIRST Saturday afternoon after New Year's Mrs. Tischler and Mrs. Gottselig came to see Mom. The reason these two heavyweight Graces — my own mother was the third! — converged on our home was as follows: Mrs. Tischler wanted to use our piano once more for teaching. I, upstairs in the "boys's" room, was irresistibly attracted downstairs by the merriment I could hear below.

Mrs. Tischler got right down to business. Ours was the best piano in Minby, she said, flattering mother a little for what was to follow. Since everyone came to Minby on Saturday anyway, she continued, it was by far most practical for her and her students to meet on Saturday in town. Mrs. Tischler had given Greta, my older sister, all the instruction she had had in return for the use of the piano. Now she was suggesting that she give one of the other Viggos lessons, "Wally, there" — pointing at me — for the use of it once more. Mom, of course, agreed, and I had my first lesson that day. I had taught myself a few bits and pieces before Mrs. Tischler entered my life, however.

Greta had taken her music books with her to college. The only music in the house now was the new Protestant Church Hymnary I was using when I played for the minister in Bethel Tabernacle, and Mrs. Tischler, a good Roman Catholic, snorted when I showed her that. Luckily she had received a brand new *Etude* in the mail only an hour before, and she hopefully unrolled it. Perhaps there was something suitable in it for me. There was. I found the little piece she picked out melodious and fascinating. I would have practiced pieces like this by the hour for her. But no — doesn't it say somewhere that man does not live by bread alone? Neither does he live on just cake, for Mrs. Tischler wrote down a list of exercises I had to play, and what she called "arpejas" too, and Heaven knows what else!

My first lesson evidently started out under the best possible auspices, because I got my first gold star before it was over. I had often seen Mrs. Tischler reach into her voluminous combination suitcase-handbag-purse and bring forth two little cardboard boxes, one with a gold star stuck on top, the other with little red and blue dots to indicate the contents.

That first lesson was typical of the half a dozen I was to receive from my teacher. She and I would both try to find room on the piano bench, her voluminous *derrière* occupying a full four-fifths of the tiny area, I precariously balancing as best I could on the little that was left over. Mrs. Tischler was shaped like an egg, and since she was sitting on the big end of it, that left me even less room than one might think.

We would get nicely started on a scale or the piece I was playing but the laughter from Mom and Mrs. Gottselig in the other room was too much for Mrs. Tischler; her curiosity always got the better of her; she would lean towards the kitchen, the better to hear, almost shoving me off my uncertain perch; she got so uneasy at times that she would stop me from playing to ask what she was missing. After she found out, we would go on a little further until the next gale of laughter pulled her attention kitchen- and coffee-wards again. Small wonder then that the meager instruction I got dragged to almost an hour that first day. Perhaps the first gold star was compensation for my patience.

The following Saturday when I played my lesson, she put another two or three gold stars on that page and being in a really colorful mood that day, she stuck on a few of the red and blue dots too. She had an extraordinary sense of proportion and balance and like Kandinsky, she knew exactly where to put these little bits of colored paper for an attractive pattern.

After half a dozen lessons in this manner, after every one of which she wrote "Excellent" diagonally across the page, corner to corner, sticking in a few more dots and stars for good measure, one Saturday came when Mrs. Tischler brought along a jar of her homemade beet relish, beet relish with a bit of sharp horseradish in it, she told me, licking her lips in anticipation. She had a big smile on her face and a glint in her eye when she brought this jar, along with her dot and star boxes, from the depths of her colossal multipurpose handbag. She was going to surprise Mom.

Mrs. Tischler had deduced, the previous week, that we were going to be butchering; she had seen Mom's preparations the Saturday before, and she knew that my mother would be making headcheese. Mom always made headcheese. When the Viggos butchered, they, like the big packing houses, utilized everything but the pig's squeal. Mrs. Tischler put her jar of beet relish on the piano right beside my music. Not that she really needed a reminder . . .

We had been seated for some minutes at the piano, and I was well into my lesson, when, from the kitchen, the tantalizing odor of percolating coffee reached us. It was too much for Mrs. Tischler — she executed a half-roll off the piano bench quicker than I thought it possible for a woman of her obesity to move. She told me to continue with my lesson.

From the kitchen, a minute later . . . "Play 'Country Dance'!"

I played "Country Dance."

"Play it again, Wally, not so fast, and watch your fingering!"

I played it once more, exactly as I had played it the first time, paying even less attention to my fingering.

"That's better! You should *allus* play it like that, *ev'y* time!"

Silence . . .

After waiting for two or three minutes for further orders and getting none — I could just hear the low murmur of their voices — I assumed that she and Mom had both forgotten me out in the parlor. I, in turn, slid off the bench and went out to the kitchen. There, heads down, these two connoisseurs, these two incorrigible *Feinschmecker,* were sitting enjoying generously buttered slices of Mom's whole wheat bread, thick succulent slabs of the cold headcheese that had been apressing out in the shed for the past few days and with them, of course, Mrs. Tischler's own incomparable beet relish.

Mrs. Tischler was bringing Mom up to date on all the scandal that had happened in Missenden as she, Mrs. Tischler, had been there the week before giving lessons. Dad and Mom had lived for a couple of years in Missenden before settling in Minby; Mom therefore knew all the people Mrs. Tischler was talking about. Mrs. Tischler was giving Mom the news that did *not* appear in the weekly *Missenden Thunderbolt.* I took a cup and saucer and poured myself a cup of coffee, buttered myself a slice of bread and joined them at the table.

That was all the lesson I had that day.

There was no lesson the next week either, although Mrs. Tischler came as usual and gave instruction to her other pupils. But she didn't forget me. She never forgot me. She always had some bit of music along, be it the current *Etude* or one of her old ones. Now and again she would ask me to play some piece of my own choosing, nod approvingly, and if that constituted a lesson, then I could say, I suppose, that I had had a lesson that week too. It was simply tacitly understood between her and

Mom that I was learning things my own way, and probably faster than if subjected to any kind of rigorous discipline, since what I liked to play I would play by the
hour, whereas if I were forced to play scales or arpeggios,
something I didn't like, I would, as Angèle our hired
girl would put it, "drag my feet," or just "play wit' the
ends of my fingers."

OF DAILY PAPERS AND
"GENTLEMAN" MAX

MRS. BARRY in the Drug Store and Telephone Exchange had about twenty regular customers for the big "city" papers. The majority of those who picked up their *Heralds, Posts* or *Leaders* each day were the old bucks of Minby, alert for any excuse to get in beside the village siren for a few minutes each day. They could, at a saving of a few dollars a year, have subscribed and had their favorite paper put in their Post Office box like all the others; but they liked to see how close they could get to this bewitching female when they came in and picked it off her counter. At five cents a day that, for these dissolute "big spenders," was dangerous, reckless and expensive living!

Of course they all knew the story about Mrs. Barry and Scoop Lowe, the Bath and Scottgate traveler, at the Old Hotel before it was finally condemned. They'd heard too, much more recently, about Marsh Crabtree, Scoop's competitor, and of their nocturnal visits, and the repercussions these extended calls had provoked at the New Hotel . . . As loyal Mrs. Barry supporters they all thought Mr. Müller had been unnecessarily harsh in the retaliatory measures he had taken and they had even gone so far, some of them, to boycott him. Oh the reprisals! Any lunches thereafter they solemnly swore to take at the Twentieth Century Cafe. It is true that their switch of patronage neither made Mr. Müller poor nor Mah Fong rich.

They could all remember vividly the details surrounding Mr. Müller's treachery, recalling with touching emotion the solidarity they had shown in Mrs. Barry's hour of trial. This incident had only added to Mrs. Barry's attraction for these would-be or has-been gay-blades. Those who were too old to misbehave in the Crabtree manner could still dream about it. Sunday was the only day one would miss seeing these old fools jockeying to catch Mrs. Barry's eye, or vying to be the happy recipient of her smile . . .

Old Man Carwardine, for reasons best known to himself, didn't have to justify his presence in the Drug Store by the purchase of a paper. He probably couldn't have read it anyway. This fact would not, nor did it, prevent him from being a long-time member of the Minby School Board. Perhaps in his capacity of oldest and longest subscriber to the Brighton Rural Telephone Line he had qualified for the privilege of sitting in the empty chair beside the telephone exchange for a quarter of an hour each day. There he would mildly intoxicate himself on the cascades of perfume exuding from Mrs. Barry's well-stacked person before he returned to his farm and his flat-chested mate.

On Saturdays he would stay an extra quarter of an hour and that would help tide him over the long weekend. Since Mr. Carwardine was over seventy, the concentrated half-hour exposure could make him quite giddy if he inadvertently kept his Saturday tryst on an empty stomach. Mr. Carwardine was a connoisseur, just like Max Harrison, one of the Minby grain buyers. There was a slight difference: since Carwardine was also the local dairy man, he could have been assumed better qualified than Max in their special field. Neither of these two breast experts, alas, could have possibly foreseen the ravages that time eventually wrought on their own wives' upper halves.

Max Harrison, aforementioned grain buyer, suffered somewhat from asthma and that was a bit troublesome considering his job. He was in the Drug Store a good half hour before the train each day and he didn't return to his elevator until much later, after the mail was sorted at the Post Office and the *Heralds, Journals* and *Leaders* brought down to the Drug Store where Mrs. Barry herself wrote on the customers' names. She could have just handed Max his copy when she undid the bundle of papers; but he waited each day while she consecrated it with his name, letter by letter, syllable by syllable, after which she would hand it to him with an indulgent, good-natured smile.

Max was transfixed by any woman with a big bosom, and since Mrs. Barry's was unquestionably the largest in Minby AND Missenden AND Culbertson, he would stare at it like a man hypnotized as she put the finishing flourish to his name. Even *I* couldn't help remarking those extraordinary proportions, like twin kettledrums, for I, too, was fascinated, not by her bosom however, but by her eyes, and to see them — big and brown, bigger and browner than Angèle's even — I had to somehow peer over those overgenerous breasts. For a kid of my height and age, that meant standing back at least eight feet . . .

Mrs. Barry was quite aware of the dangers her feminine charms presented to Mr. Harrison's troubled respiration. If she was in a playful mood, if the telephone switchboard wasn't too busy, and if "Gentleman" Max was standing at the proper place at the counter, she was known to get up and move in closer than usual to him, tease him by leaning over and exposing just a little more of her rotund treasures than usual, which would send poor asthmatic Max, red-faced and hand in pocket to the door, gasping for air as if someone had thrust a bouquet of pollen-laden flowers under his nose.

Why then, when he had asthma so bad, did Max Harrison run an elevator for a living? The answer was quite simple: he didn't have asthma when he arrived in

Minby in 'fourteen. It was something that had crept up on him over the past decade and a half and which was aggravated by the environment in which he worked. Moreover, after spending the best years of his life in this pursuit, what else could he do? Fortunately, in the busy fall season of late, his company had been giving him an experienced "second man" when the grain came in and when he had to load. Barney Grant, a fellow countryman, who operated the Pool Hall, gave him a hand when he had nothing else to do. During the winter when he was by himself he could handle things quite capably alone. If necessary, however, he would call on one of his "competitors," the other elevator men, when he needed help moving a car, or mixing and loading grain.

If Old Jack Smythe was first into Minby each year with a load of threshed wheat, Max could bask in the reflected glory, for it was his elevator which received it. Max would carefully note the grade, calculate the probable yield per acre for him, and turn that information over to the Lobb girls. They, in turn, saw to it that it got into the next week's *Missenden Thunderbolt* and, on occasion, into the city papers as well. Max had his loyal customers who stuck by him in his infirmity — certainly the most fervent of whom was Old Jack. Naturally Max reciprocated by publicizing far and wide and loyally upholding the now time-hallowed Smythe traditions, the annual corn feed, and the more exclusive tripe banquet which followed a week or two later. Old Jack would slyly rib Max about his asthma, ask, with a twinkle in his eye, if it interfered with his love life . . . This would cause the tip of Max's nose to glow a soft red.

Of course everybody knew — with the possible exception of Max's own flat-chested wife — about his penchant for big-bosomed females. Why shouldn't they have known when he did so little to conceal his interest himself? Everybody was just as persuaded that if the opportunity presented itself for Max to indulge his passion, he would throw up his hands and run. In other words, the consensus was that "Gentleman" Max was *indeed* a gentleman and not, like Old Jack, a man of action. Old Jack, however — certain of the Minbyites credited him with second sight (after all wasn't he almost a dowser himself after all these years?) — didn't share the general assessment of his long-time business associate.

Max was English and prided himself on it. He "bought British" before it became a national slogan and had, ever since his arrival in Minby, sent back to the London stores for every article of apparel he and his wife wore. No Eaton's or Simpson's for them! It was public knowledge, too, that he had a scandalously extravagant vice and that the large package which he received approximately every three months was his quarterly supply of English pipe tobacco which was available nowhere in the province. It was red-letter day if the expected consignment didn't arrive on schedule and Max was reduced to one of his old discarded pipes and the local tobacco, for *never* would he contaminate his "good" pipes with the domestic brands. He had meerschaum pipes as old and as mellow as Reverend Keynes', and it was a big event when Reverend Keynes arrived in Minby and Max could offer his fellow Britisher and connoisseur a pipeful of his specially imported English mixture. Indeed there was a touch of class, a smack of "Old England" in Barney Grant's Pool Hall and Barber Shop when *both* meerschaums were filled and glowing as Reverend Keynes and "Gentleman" Max, two *billiard* experts, played their weekly match — weekly, that is, until Mrs. Red Blaine put an abrupt halt to the Reverend's dissipation.

As a further indication of Max's thoroughgoing loyalty to the Mother Country, he had been a most voluble supporter of Lionel Stephenson's perpetual motion machine. Was it because he thought no Englishman could be the fool Lionel at times appeared to be? Or was Max simply one of Lionel's backers in his wondrous dream of one day "inventing perpetual motion plus power"? English to the core, both Mr. and Mrs. Harrison planned for the day when Max would shut the big doors of the elevator for good and when they could retire to the land of their fathers. Had Max been hoping to supplement his savings from Lionel's dream-come-true? Perhaps . . . Ah — good old England! If Max knew no other lines of poetry, he knew those of Browning that went "Oh to be in England now that April's there." More than one Minbyite had heard him repeat that profound wish when the snow was leaving and the first larks of spring were beginning to be heard.

Max was the epitome of regularity. "His" farmers knew that his elevator was open promptly at seven when no one else's was, winter and summer alike. They knew, too, that when he wasn't at his elevator, he could be found at the Drug Store, this *invariably* from train time until he picked up his daily paper from Mrs. Barry. For the rest of the time when he wasn't busy, he pretended that he was, sitting at his desk from where he could look out the north window and see all activity at the station platform.

Looking out the west window straight in front of him he could check on everyone coming from or going to the depot since that was the only crossing; with the door of his office open looking south, he could see everything going up or down Main Street; most important, he could fondly gaze across into Mrs. Barry's Drug Store which had such a warm spot in his affections . . . The only direction cut off from his view was east: his office had no window on that side — but then his elevator was in the way and, anyway, who came into Minby from that end of town except whoever happened to be squatting on the "Old Pringle Place"?

In short, Max was aware of everything going on. He was as up to date on Minby's pulsating life as Old Scott McEachern, but with this difference: Max's curiosity would never permit him to cruise around the village soliciting or divulging gossip; and Old Scott had long ago given up calling at Max's office for information that he knew Max could give but wouldn't.

His work over, Max's departure for home didn't vary a minute from day to day except in the busy season. Still later in the day the rummy hounds in the Pool Hall and Barber Shop knew they could set their watches at 9 p.m. when he came in and, if they were too intent on their game, they had another chance at 9.30 when he said "Good night, gentlemen" and left for home. His evening promenade was more a circular tour of the village — he would come down the boardwalk along Main Street as far as the Pool Hall, leaving that building, his visit terminated, by the rear to take the back lane home.

Max wasn't referred to as "Gentleman" Max for nothing although it is true that he had a ready ear for any dirty story being related during his 9 to 9.30 halt at the Pool Hall. "Uncle" Martin, Minby's specialist in this *genre*, and Jack Fender, a close second, both made it a point to hold their ripest and choicest obscenities in abeyance until he appeared. It was their avowed intention to make him blush, just once, but they never succeeded. If, pipe in mouth, he listened casually, albeit attentively, he was *never* known to reciprocate. Neither would he disdain to listen to the choice bits of gossip circulating about the fairer sex — he'd even smile indulgently at the frailty of woman but *never* would he contribute an uncavalierly remark nor press for more details. That was rarely necessary anyway: if details were lacking or somewhat vague, wasn't there always another more curious than he to solicit them in his place? Only once was he annoyed, sufficiently annoyed as a matter of fact to avoid the Pool Hall for close to a month, only resuming his nocturnal visits when he had to have his next haircut. That was when Old Stewart, who frequented that place about the least of any, stared him in the face and pointedly asked him why he didn't take his walks in broad daylight like anyone else instead of prowling around after dark.

Max, in spite of his age — he was crowding sixty — was an ardent dancer. Dancing was the God-given opportunity he needed to legitimately snuggle up to the buxom females of Minby and he utilized it to the full. He would have the first dance, the Supper Waltz, and any Ladies' choice waltzes that might come in between these two with his wife; but for all the others, he saw to it that at least one of the partner-less women had an escort, passing from one replete female to the next, dancing with "Hann' " Kripps and Mrs. Barry and any other widow present more than once in the course of the evening. One-steps and fox-trots — he could dance them all. If "Big Bertha" sat out every dance except those in which she asked her cousin Daisy, her inseparable side-kick and fellow spinster, she could be sure of having at least one dance with "Gentleman" Max. For a man whose asthma was as bad as Max's unquestionably was, an evening of this nature could be considered quite an achievement.

How shocked after the Live Wires' concert, at which they performed "Cinderella," and the dance that followed was Minby to hear that Max had collapsed on his way to open his elevator at seven o'clock the following morning. Nothing in his behavior the night before indicated he wasn't long for this world. The same day Frank Laidlaw, his superintendent, arrived on the four o'clock from the city to check the books and to arrange for a temporary replacement. His books, so Mr. Laidlaw said, were in order, meticulously in order, as only Max could have kept them.

"Uncle" Martin and Jack Fender had dropped by at the elevator office just as Mr. Laidlaw was unsuccessfully trying to open the last and largest drawer of all. What could be in it? And why was it locked? And where was the key? If it was company business, the superintendent wanted to know about it, but now was hardly the time to go up and bother his widow about it.

"Uncle" Martin and Jack, always the ready helpers, particularly when it meant satisfying their own curiosity, had the lock picked in less than two minutes with the aid of an "Old Horn" beer bottle opener and jackknife. Imagine their amazement, and the superintendent's, and the whole community's when "Gentleman" Max's depravity became common knowledge ("Uncle" Martin and Jack Fender were hardly the sort to keep such a tidbit to themselves . . .). Filed away — for indeed it was a drawer meant for filing — were no less than thirty-five pairs of women's panties, of every size and color, all date-tagged and with identifying initials that only Max, the author, (or the original owners, perhaps) might have deciphered, panties and step-ins and one voluminous pair of bloomers that went back to 1915 that he had patiently gathered and hoarded over the years. And on top, the most recent of all, that very special pair, those red ones with the white lace trimmings that had disappeared the night of the Wheat Pool movie when the Spanish *danseuse* had given her solo.

Mrs. Barry, directly across the street, left her switchboard just long enough to run over and positively identify seven of the thirty-five as hers. No other woman in Minby was that eager to satisfy her own — and the rest of the community's — curiosity about the others.

EXIT FRIEDRICH SCHALLER

"WANT to come along, Wally?"

"Where to?"

"If I told you, you wouldn't want to go!"

It was Mr. Stewart who picked me up this Saturday afternoon. We had spent all morning in Saturday School at Reverend Kreuz's house. I had just had dinner and with nothing else to do hopped in beside him in his big Hudson. In addition to being Hudson dealer — he never sold one, but being their agent it permitted him to drive a big limousine around at wholesale price — Mr. Stewart was one of Minby's machine agents too. His store had begun as a hardware store under his predecessor, but he added a line of groceries which had now invaded almost all the original premises. Mr. Stewart had the B.A. Oil Agency and two B.A. gas pumps in front of his store. He sold a carload of binder twine every fall, and even a bit of hail insurance when he had the chance to make a call.

One would hesitate to call Mr. Stewart the local undertaker. Most of the Minbyites passed away in the Missenden hospital and there was a *funeral parlor* up there . . . If it was something "real bad," they passed on in the city from where they were shipped home in a coffin all ready for burial.

There were a good many Minby people who would postpone dying as long as they could, or take the train to the city hospital at the threat of a serious illness if they thought Mr. Stewart would be the last one to handle them. No one, in other words, was dying to have him for their undertaker.

It was in Mr. Stewart's part-time occupation as mortician that he was heading out south this afternoon but he didn't tell me right away. He didn't even tell me that anyone had died. Nor did this man just die . . . Mr. Stewart enjoyed his little joke right to the end, right up until we drove into Schaller's farmyard, pulling up in front of the house.

"Schaller committed suicide," he said as casually as if he were discussing a mild change in the weather. Perhaps he didn't want to scare me, "and we're going to fix him up," he added with cozy emphasis on the "we."

Suicide? I stiffened a bit when he said that. How come I hadn't heard about that in town? And what did he mean by *"we're* going to fix him up"?

It still wasn't common knowledge in Minby that Mr. Schaller had committed suicide. Only two or three hours earlier the police had pulled him out of the well after being notified by his neighbors that they hadn't seen him around for a few days, and that the cattle were bawling and kicking up a ruckus in the barn because they hadn't been fed, milked or watered.

Mr. Schaller's farm was like so many of the farms around Minby. The buildings consisted of a huge, well-painted red barn with neat white trim. About a hundred yards from it, however, was a small unpainted shack of a house to which we were now heading. There was an unpainted outhouse too, of course, and a couple of granaries. Of trees or shrubs to break the monotony, not a trace . . .

The police had left the house locked, and since Mr. Stewart didn't have a key, he jimmied the first loose window he could open and shoved me in. I was to open one of the doors from the inside. I had evidently landed in the "good room." All the farm houses I had been in had a "good room."

I found my way to the kitchen, passed what looked to be pans of bread dough covered with a sheet set to raise on the kitchen table. Didn't Mom always cover her "sponge" that way? I pulled back the bolt of the kitchen door and let Mr. Stewart in. When I turned around again and was once more facing my port of entry I could see the dirty soles of Mr. Schaller's bare feet now visible to me from under the sheet. His naked corpse was stretched out on the table, just as the police had left it after undressing it before noon.

"Pretty, isn't he?" said Old Stewart gruffly.

Mr. Stewart seemed to hesitate as to where he should start. Finally he pulled down the top part of the sheet thus exposing the head, the heavy, matted black hair, and the thick dark beard of the dead man.

I was scared and fascinated at the same time. I had never seen a dead person before and took comfort in the fact that Mr. Stewart was along in the kitchen beside me. But to get closer to this "comfort," Mr. Stewart — I had to get closer to the body too. I preferred to stay where I was, a respectable distance away.

I went outside after a bit to get away from the corpse, but was irresistibly drawn back after only a few minutes. My reason told me there was absolutely nothing to be afraid of, much less to be afraid of in fact than some of the *live* people I happened to know in the district. So I watched Mr. Stewart prepare the body. Prayers were to be said that night, and it had to be presentable.

Mr. Stewart had me look for scissors and when I found a pair he set to work snipping off the bulk of the heavy beard and trimming as much as he could of the unkempt shock of black hair.

Mr. Schaller looked exceedingly black all the time, having a dark reddish-blue, almost purple complexion. I never once saw him really clean-shaven. He lived a long way out and always drove in with a team and wagon;

maybe his beard was so thick and grew so fast that he had five o'clock shadow by the time he arrived in town. Probably he had quit shaving altogether after his wife left him.

Snipping off what beard he could with the scissors, Mr. Stewart opened a fresh pack of Gillette blades to give him a dry shave. The silence in the kitchen was only interrupted by the periodic rumbling from Mr. Stewart's insides on the one hand and the steady scraping of the razor blades like striking a match on sandpaper, on the other. Slowly Mr. Schaller's face came to light.

Mr. Schaller, who could have been sleeping on the kitchen table, looked less like a corpse than Old Stewart did who was cleaning him up. Mr. Stewart was certainly ten or fifteen years younger than he looked; but he had chronic stomach trouble, chewed tobacco incessantly, and since I never once saw him spit, I always fancied that that was why he looked so yellow, and that the intermittent and distinctly audible rumblings from his stomach were his digestive organs protesting against the massive intake of nicotine.

Mr. Stewart's complexion was a yellow-tan and even the whites of his eyes were yellowish; his false teeth were a yellow brown from the tobacco, right up to the orange-brown part that was to represent the gums. He was practically bald, with just a tiny narrow fringe of hair at the back of his head, and the top of his head was the color of an old ivory billiard ball; today, however, his head wasn't visible at all; for sheer deviltry Mr. Stewart had tied a dish towel around it, one that he had found hanging on Schaller's kitchen stove when he entered the house. He guffawed at his own joke when he said that the towel kept the hair out of his eyes.

As Schaller's face became visible, I could see that he wasn't old at all. Maybe he was only about thirty or thirty-five, or younger. Mr. Stewart interrupted his shaving two or three times to rest his hand and to clear the whiskers out of the way as he put in a fresh razor blade. Several times he lifted up the corpse's right arm to let it fall heavily again on the table by the body. It fascinated him. He pointed out to me that Mr. Schaller had probably broken that shoulder in his jump to the bottom of the well. Perhaps it had hit some projection on the way down. *Rigor mortis* had long ago set in, and it was a fact that the other arm scarcely gave under Mr. Stewart's attempts to show the different reactions of the two.

According to what the police told Mr. Stewart, Mrs. Schaller had blamed her husband for their boy's death the previous August, saying God was punishing him because he didn't go to church. Schaller must have been planning his suicide for a long time then, Mr. Stewart concluded, probably ever since his wife packed up their two little girls and took them with her to the States.

It was at that very moment, as if to show Mr. Stewart that his conjectures were all wrong, that I, because of my usual curiosity, opened the oven door of the kitchen range. I was not surprised to see a roaster in it. Didn't Mom habitually leave her roaster, bread pans and cookie sheets in the oven too where they were out of the way but handy? I pulled this roaster out on to the oven door, and took the lid off.

Old Stewart's face took on a look of complete bewilderment when he saw the perfectly edible roast chicken that was in it, drumsticks pointing outwards and upwards in the best roast chicken tradition. All he could say was "Well I'll be damned." And two minutes later, "I'll be go to hell!"'

That knocked Mr. Stewart's and the police's theories into a cocked hat. Was this a coldly calculated suicide after all? It is possible that Mr. Schaller no longer thought life worth living. Perhaps he had received a certain bit of bad news, unexpectedly, which had been sufficient to precipitate his drastic act. Or had he, like King Tut, prepared a little snack for his departure into the other world?

While Mr. Stewart and I were discussing this, Frank Kupf drove up in his buggy to see what was going on. Kupf's farm was just half a mile east of Schaller's. Although belonging to the same church, although neighbors and of the same racial extraction, Mr. Schaller, Kupf pointed out, didn't "neighbor" with him much. To set the record straight, it was common knowledge that if Kupf was ready to "neighbor," as he described it, a good many of his neighbors would have preferred that he didn't. His way of neighboring was very one-sided, running one way, like a one-way street, *his* way . . .

Mr. Stewart told me on the way home that Kupf had probably only driven in to see what he could pick up. No doubt wanting to profit by Mr. Kupf's presence in the kitchen with him, Mr. Stewart brought in Mr. Schaller's suit from the next room, asking Mr. Kupf if he would mind helping him dress up his dead neighbor. Mr. Stewart still wasn't quite finished the job of shaving, but he could complete that later. Mr. Kupf apparently *did* mind helping, which was clear from the startled look on his face when he heard Mr. Stewart's request.

"Just a minute," he stammered, went out, and after a long five minutes came back from his buggy wearing a pair of gloves. Mr. Kupf might have shaken hands with Mr. Schaller a day or two earlier when he was still alive, barehanded, but today he wasn't taking any chances.

I couldn't help thinking of Angèle, our hired girl, and how she expressed herself in English. If there was something we didn't like to eat, something we just nibbled at, then she said that we ate "wit' the ends of our teet'." That would describe how Mr. Kupf helped Mr. Stewart dress Mr. Schaller. All he used were the ends of his fingers, and wearing gloves at that. That job done, he took his hasty departure, fearing no doubt that he might be asked to give further assistance.

Mr. Stewart made short work of the rest of the cleaning-up operations and we left via the kitchen, pulling the door shut behind us. We didn't bother locking it up.

"He won't be going any place," said Mr. Stewart dryly, taking an enormously big chew from his plug of tobacco.

A final check and we hopped into the Hudson and headed for Minby.

News of Schaller's suicide hadn't any more than broken in town. Someone in the family started telling *me* about it as I came in the door. Imagine with what gusto I answered that *I* had been helping Mr. Stewart get him ready for the funeral!

I put on a big show then, but I had a change of tone about an hour afterwards. Mom, who evidently feared pollution as much as Mr. Kupf did, told me first of all to "get right over to the sink, kid, and *scrub* yourself." I did. Then she reminded to "get right up to the church" and practice my hymns. I grabbed the Hymnal and ran.

It was a good deal later than I thought. Day was already finishing. By the time I got to the little Tabernacle and up to the organ it was too dark to see my music. At least that's what I told Mom when I came running home. For while I was seated there in the semi-darkness, ruminating on the events I had witnessed in the Schaller kitchen only a few hours before, and thinking of the dozens of corpses over which funeral services had been held in this very building, a block of wood or a lump of coal in the basement beneath me chose the most inauspicious moment to roll down the pile on to the floor, setting other blocks of wood and coal into motion too, and that scared the living daylights out of me.

For some reason my mind focused on Mr. Schaller lying cold and stiff on his kitchen table just as we had left him. For the same reason, perhaps, I expected him, like Lazarus, to get up and come out of one of the gloomy corners of the darkening building and to come up to me with his icy hands. I sat stiff as a rod, goose pimples over my whole body. Then, when a ghostly shadow flitted noiselessly past the windowpane only a few yards from where I was sitting I gave one terrified yell and knocked over the stool in my haste to get out of the church. The Hymnal I left on the organ. Nothing, absolutely nothing could make me go back in and get it. I would have to do my practicing early the next morning, before church. ·

THE STRAP

MR. DORRITT, my first teacher, reminded me of Santa Claus because of his gray-white beard. He used to pass our house every day on his way to school. But if when I was a preschooler of five he resembled *Saint* Nick, he approximated *Old* Nick even more closely the next year when I started Grade One. He looked much older than he was in reality. Perhaps the increasing school enrollment had aged him. Along with too many pupils in too many grades, he had too many obstreperous "big kids," part-time farm boy pupils who came in only during the winter months.

How had he been able to give us beginners the time and attention we needed? I learned my ABC's, did simple arithmetic, receiving a thorough grounding. But I "dragged my feet," as Angèle would say, when I had to read page after page about the Little Red Hen, perhaps the most stupid tale ever concocted for child education. "You would not help me cut the wheat, you would not help me make the bread, you shall not eat the bread, my little chicks shall eat the bread, and they did." The inanity, vapidity and insipidity of this selection were exceeded only by the story *Little Half Chick*.

Everything was done in such a strict, business-like, no fooling manner that I "crept like a snail unwillingly to school" every morning and afternoon because once our work was done, woe betide us if we were caught doing anything else not related to our assignments. Thereafter, as long as I had Mr. Dorritt for a teacher I dawdled over my work to prolong it; I drew my words more than I wrote them, and when finished, I just sat and waited, waited and sat. Yet Mr. Dorritt did one thing regularly which indicated he had a heart after all; he let us beginners out at three o'clock instead of keeping us till three thirty with the rest.

I wasn't fooling Mr. Dorritt when I dawdled, because busy as he was, he could see that I was idle much of the time. On my first report he wrote: "Waldemar is a little indolent." Mama beamed when she passed it over to Mrs. Haugen at four o'clock coffee, thinking that Mr. Dorritt meant that her boy, her Wally, was a little angel, the "indolent" being an English adjective she still hadn't encountered. Mrs. Haugen, ever one to keep things in proper perspective where their respective progeny was concerned, made the required correction.

I got my first licking in school from Mr. Dorritt the very week I started. One of the "big kids" had thrown a paper glider. All pupils, since time immemorial, have made these gliders from a torn-out scribbler page. This glider had come out of nowhere ever so gracefully to make a perfect three-point landing on my side of the wide double-desk I shared with my older brother Kalle, who was in Grade Three. It had been destined for him — he would have known what to do with it. Before he had time to hide it or return it, I had it in my hand and sent it back in the same direction. What fun! School wasn't so bad after all! It hit Mr. Dorritt — a perfect bull's eye. He had no difficulty identifying the culprit, for I was still proudly watching the path the missile had taken in its silent flight, quite enthusiastic with the results of my first launching, but confident I'd do *much* better with my next.

Mr. Dorritt gave no first or second˘warnings. He lifted me out of my desk by the ear and led me up to his own at the front of the room where he picked up his strap. He had had it ready. This strap was very original, one he had *manufactured* himself. It consisted of three pieces of inner tube, two gray-black and one red

in between the two (he liked symmetry . . .) each about
an inch wide by eighteen inches long; these three lengths
of rubber were ignobly tied together with a piece of vulgar
grocery string. The licking which he administered in sight
of all the other pupils didn't hurt physically, nor was
it meant to; but I was flushed with shame and mortifica-
tion, for I had been the first to get it that fall, the very
first.

The fact that I was new to school, six, the youngest
of the lot didn't make any difference. He made an example early every term to "put the fear of Dorritt" into
the rest of the kids — I happened to be "it" that year.
I got another licking at home, that one from an expert.

That strapping five years before from Mr. Dorritt
had been deserved and I never held anything against
him or my father afterwards. The one this week from
Mr. Mitchell, on the contrary, was in a different category.
I had so little to do in school that boredom, nothing
but boredom, was the cause of my misfortune.

We would have had plenty to do with an organized
teacher to guide us; but with Mr. Mitchell I seldom had
anything to turn to and literally ached with ennui trying
to put in the time. I wasn't the only one — the faces
of my schoolmates indicated that they would have preferred something to do too. I had no talents as an artist,
but for lack of anything better, I filled most of my scribblers and the inside covers of my textbooks with nonsen-
sical sketches. I had picked up an old library book one day
too, and on the flyleaf someone had written: "If my name
you want to see, turn to page one hundred and three."
I turned to page 103 where I read: "If my name you
do not find, shut the book and never mind." That gave
me an idea, and I took my history text and made cross
references of a similar poetical nature on *every* page of
it. If only I had doodled away keeping my head down,
pretending to work, all would have been well. But isn't

pretending to work even harder than performing a real task?

I was looking back at red-headed Christina Blaine. We had been warned many times against leaving our drawer pulled out in case Mr. Mitchell or one of the other pupils coming down the aisle should walk into it. That is not what happened; but when I leaned around to see Christina, the desk overbalanced, tottered for a moment to finally topple over because of my overhanging weight and the weight of the books in the drawer. There was a mighty crash followed by a few more seconds' disturbance as I tried to right myself.

I had interrupted Mr. Mitchell. In a flash he was beside me, jerking me by my collar. I still hadn't had time to get up on my feet.

"Into the library!"

Without waiting for me to set up my desk again, he dragged me more than I walked the first few yards. And so into the library, he banging the door shut behind us. That boded no good.

Of course Mr. Mitchell had punished one or two of the kids before me, one of whom was Bert Kaschl. When Dad heard that he told us grimly that if we couldn't behave any better than the Kaschl kids and got a licking in school, we knew what we could expect when we got home. I got goose pimples at the menace in Dad's voice, though I knew or thought at the time that that could never happen to me. Mr. Mitchell had obviously had all he could take that day — my little accident had been the proverbial last straw.

"Hold out your hands!" he said, already crimson in the face.

I held out my hands, stiff as a board. Hadn't Bert Kaschl told us that it wouldn't hurt as much if you held your hands out this way? Bert also said that rubbing the palms with orange peel took away the sting; but I didn't have any orange peel and Mr. Mitchell didn't look as if he would give me time out for that anyway.

I stood fearfully, arms outstretched, beside the brand new library table, in this lovely new library room that I had so eagerly watched under construction the summer before. Mr. Mitchell impatiently opened one drawer after the other until he found his strap. It was in the third and last, and he became more on edge and his face more and more flushed after slamming the first two shut again.

Mr. Mitchell's strap was a piece of ordinary belting about two inches wide and about twenty inches long, a piece of everyday machine shop belting that could be picked up in Stewart's hardware store. It was a dirty gray, about 3/16'' thick with a somewhat silverish white line about half an inch wide running down the whole length of it.

It was hard to believe that the Mr. Mitchell standing in front of me now was the same man I had seen swinging Miss Chatwin, the grades One to Three teacher, around at the dance only a few nights before. I wondered if he would really strap me with that ugly piece of belt. Would he stand at right angles to me and whack me *across* my palm? Holding the belt firmly by the last three inches of it with the right hand, he began to strap me so that I got the full length of it on my palms and right up the arms.

The first two or three lashes hurt the most. How many times he hit me altogether I couldn't say but I do remember hoping each one would be the last. I resolved not to cry and that obviously irritated him. Twice in succession he missed me and hit himself across the knee. Thinking, no doubt, I had moved my arms out of the way, he became furious and the blows fell hot and heavy until, exhausted, purple in the face, his long pompadour hair hanging down incongruously on both sides of his flushed face, he said in a croak of a voice,

"Get to hell back to your seat!" He was shaking all over and could hardly get the words out of his mouth.

I returned to the strangely quiet room. The other pupils had heard all the ruckus, the walls between the classroom and the library being anything but soundproof. I tried to smile, but it didn't quite come off. No one stirred for fear he or she would be next.

It took a full five minutes for Mr. Mitchell to pull himself together, comb his hair, and come back to his students. He went directly to his desk, sat down and didn't utter another word for the rest of the period, the last one for the day. No one stirred.

Now I didn't want school to come to an end because I was afraid to go home; and yet I couldn't wait for three thirty to come so I could get out of the schoolroom and look at my arms, which were so stiff that I could hardly move them. My eczema bandages were as taut as if they had been tied on like the wet leather thongs the Indians reputedly used on their victims: as these thongs dried, they were supposed to get tighter still . . .

I didn't shed a single tear in school; but before I reached home I was sobbing a bit to myself. Louis Kovacz had caught up to me and was trying to comfort me, and it was his sympathy and his tears more than anything else that finally made mine come. When I saw Mom standing in the kitchen, quite unprepared for what I had to tell her, then I really cried.

"What's the matter, kid?"

"I got a licking at school!"

"You what!" said Mom, who heard me quite distinctly the first time. "What for?"

"I don't know!"

"What do you mean you don't know? What did Mr. Mitchell give you a licking for?"

I was crying too hard to do any explaining, and I was trying to get at the buttons of my sleeves.

"And quit trying to scratch your eczema. Dad'll give you something that'll make you itch . . ."

That was all Mom had to say to open the floodgates. When she finally got my sleeves up and my bandages untangled, she was horrified and crying worse than I. In spite of the padding from the shirt sleeves, and from several layers of gauze and ointment, every welt was visible from the wrist up the whole arm. Both arms were already black and blue down the middle, with a sickly yellow-brown tinge along the sides which was turning a dirty green color beneath our very eyes. Undoubtedly unbandaging them had allowed more blood to flow to them too, because — unless it was my imagination — they really hurt more now than they had in school. May it have been Mom's contagious tears? She cried, and I had never seen her cry like this before and that made me cry all the more.

Half dragging me after her, Mom took me out to the shop to show Dad what that awful Mr. Mitchell had done to "their" Waldemar. Of course he would be every bit as indignant as she!

Dad was at his forge, his heavy black leather apron protecting him from the flying sparks. It was not too light where he was working, and the noise of the big engine firing away driving the triphammer, of the blowers on the forges and the other machines, all but completely covered Mom's voice. All Dad heard was the tail end of her litany:

"Our Waldemar got an awful licking from Mr. Mitchell at school!"

"WHAT," thundered my Dad, pulling the share out of the fire, dropping it and his tongs on to the floor where they wouldn't burn, and he came over to where the two of us were standing.

Before Mom or I could show him my bruised arms, he had me over his knee and he began to spank me.

Had it been possible, he would have pulled my trousers down to let me have it on the bare behind; but even through the denim I felt every callous of his work-hardened hand as he drove home his truths.

"Didn't . . . I . . . say . . . . . . How . . . often . . ."

"Ingve! *Ingve! INGVE!!!*"

Dad finally let up.

"You just wait, Ingve!" were Mom's last words, and she and I, both bawling, went back to the house.

I cried. I cried as I hadn't cried in many a year. I cried as I hadn't cried since I was a baby. I wasn't crying because I had been hurt, and I was quite aware of it at the time. I conceded that Mr. Mitchell *might* have had the right to give me some kind of punishment, but not to the extent he did. The biggest blow of all was to have received a second licking from my father whom I had always considered absolutely just, strict at times, to be sure, but absolutely above reproach. Perhaps it had been one of his bad days too, just as it had undoubtedly been a bad one for Mr. Mitchell.

Mom told me to undress. No one was to see me looking like that! My school clothes were filthy black from contact with Dad's dirty blacksmith clothes; one side of my face was just as dirty as his — no doubt from rubbing against his leather apron as he held me over his knee.

Once in a tub of cold water my black and blue marks shone in all their glory. What a sight to behold! The initial shock and pain now over, I began to revel in being the martyr I felt I was! I was as proud of the marks on my arms as an infantry company is proud of its regimental colors, and my arms remained multicolored, like the dark end of the rainbow, for many days afterwards.

The first morning, and the morning thereafter, though it was still only April, Mom sent me to school in a short-sleeved summer shirt and without my customary bandages.

"Your eczema can wait for a few days, kid. Let that Mr. Mitchell have a good look at the job he did on you — do you hear?"

That's what Mom said . . .

Wasn't Mom just as anxious that my Dad see my arms too? Didn't she want him to admit that *for once* he might have been a little hasty? Perhaps. But if she and Dad, or if Dad and Mr. Mitchell ever discussed my licking again I never got to hear about it.

THE ALBATROSS

Willard PIERCE was tall for his age, woefully thin, always in need of a haircut, and with a troublesome cowlick which made his untidiness appear even worse. He always wore overalls, a faded blue shirt and, like the Kaschls, went barefoot. Willard's Dad had come up from the States fifteen years earlier, married one of the Minby belles and settled down to farm. Finding mechanical work much more to his liking, and after a fruitless decade and a half on his quarter, he, like two or three other families that year — 1929 — decided to move into Minby.

The shambles Gene Dempsey had called his workshop, half-filled with motors and broken-down cars he hadn't been able to repair, became vacant when Gene quit it to farm, and Willard's Dad decided to take it over. Besides calling himself a mechanic, Mr. Pierce bought junk, beer bottles, scrap iron, old batteries, and radiators. He wasn't much of a mechanic either though somewhat more gifted than Gene. Willard took after his Dad. The Pierces had a McLaughlin-Buick seven-passenger touring, similar in every respect to the five-year old 1924 model my Dad drove, except that theirs was even older. This, Mr. Pierce had ignobly cut down and converted into a truck shortly after his move to Minby, using it for his weekly trip to the city when he disposed of his junk. We at school always knew when such a trip had been made, for Willard, his brother and two sisters always showed up next day with some cheap trinket their mother had brought back for them from the "Five and Ten."

Willard became my friend for a while when he confided to me one day that he was building an airplane.

Actually it was only a glider but he persisted in "ennobling" it. Until then Willard hadn't provoked any particular interest in me. I had my chores to do and my hymns to practice at Bethel Tabernacle; Willard, too, had his chores and he carried water for Mrs. Barry in the telephone exchange. It was only several evenings later that we could finally slip through the sliding front door of the old garage, squeeze past the car bodies and dismantled engines Gene had left behind, to reach the workbench at the rear. There was an indescribable clutter of junk and very little room for anyone to stand and work. Everywhere I looked there were pigeon droppings, the stench of which was overpowering and I could hear the pigeons cooing and rustling above me. The first thing Willard grabbed was his old straw hat. No wonder! It was a precaution well worth taking — he never wore one otherwise.

"There," he said proudly, pointing to what looked like an elongated open box made of one-by-twos and slats from banana crates. It was about ten feet long, with the wheel of a baby buggy on an axle on the top of one end.

Should I show my ignorance and confess I could make neither head nor tail of it? Wasn't "tail" the proper term for one end — for if it **was** a plane, wouldn't it have to have a tail?

Noting my perplexity, and happy to volunteer an explanation, Willard enlightened me. Willard who was absolutely tongue-tied in class on the rare occasion Mr. Mitchell asked him a question was as voluble now as Einstein illustrating his Theory of Relativity.

"What you're lookin' at, Wally, is the fuselage. Of course it's upside down . . ."

That, evidently, explained why the wheel appeared to be on top.

"But shouldn't you have *two* wheels?" I ventured

cautiously, beginning to see some design after all, although his fuselage didn't taper away to much of a tail.

"It'd be better with two, but when it's centered it'll balance like a bike, so it really *don't* matter — I'll on'y need it takin' off and landin'. Besides I on'y got the one . . ."

He'd only need it taking off and landing! *That* I had to see!

"What are you going to cover it with?" I asked.

"Gunny sackin'." And he pointed to piles of gunny sacks which his Dad had already accumulated as a by-product of his feed-grinding and milling side-line.

"But the wind'll go right through it," I said critically, remembering the paper-thin, airtight, shellacked fabric of a real plane I'd seen.

"Oh, I got that all figured out. I've started savin' brown wrappin' paper. I'll cover it first with that, that'll make it airtight, and the sackin' over top'll keep it from rippin'."

I was sure it would never fly but it wasn't to humor Willard that I kept my doubts to myself. After all he was thirteen, two years older than I. But I was curious about a number of things now, not the least of which was what the finished product would be like — how he'd fasten the wings to the fuselage, how he'd build the tail and, more important, how he'd control his "ship" once in flight.

"What'cha callin' it?"

"The *Albatross*," beamed Willard.

Convinced, superconvinced even that Willard's *Albatross* would never get off the ground, I nevertheless promised him a hand when I could. Our recesses thereafter were lively discussions on aerodynamics, Willard explaining his theories of flight with hastily drawn sketches, much in the manner of Leonardo da Vinci four centuries earlier . . .

The two of us scavenged bits of lumber anywhere we could, finishing nails and spikes from my Dad's shop; when "Uncle" Martin heard what we were up to, he good-humoredly gave us an old package of glue with the understanding he was to have a ride when the plane was *operational* . . . All this material found its way to Pierces' garage. An old motto dating from the days when Gene Dempsey was still its proprietor hung on the wall. It read, "Work like Helen B. Happy" and indeed Willard worked like a man possessed — only Lionel Stephenson, Minby's inventor, at his perpetual-motion-plus-power machine was more assiduous than Willard at his *Albatross*.

Why, if I knew Willard's craft would never fly, did I keep going down to his place to help? Why didn't I point out to him that his was an unrealizable dream? Simply because I had promised . . . With his projected take-off now only days away — he had everything just about completed, braced, glued, covered with paper and sacking — wouldn't it have been kinder to say he shouldn't risk his life in his *Albatross* when it was obvious it wouldn't fly. I worriedly hoped Willard would see the impossibility of his dream and gracefully give up his project before breaking his neck, for he was planning to launch it from what we still called Max Harrison's grain elevator, although Max was no longer with us. But Willard only got all the more feverish in his excitement as the big day approached, the gleam in his eye now resembling Lionel Stephenson's when Lionel spoke about starting up his perpetual motion machine.

Indeed I had made Willard my promise. That global commitment would include helping him get his craft up to the top of Max's elevator, reassembling it for flight. Willard had more than just toyed with that idea but, his guardian angel be praised, he gave it up — not however because he thought it dangerous *per se,* but simply because, as he said himself, if he launched his glider to the east or to the west, he would hit one of the other elevators in line with Max's before he had enough speed to clear them. And if he took off facing south and was forced to land, the chances were he'd end up on the roof of Mrs. Barry's drug store, or, worse still, on one of the churches. "And they all got sharp steeples," he said with a grin. And if he headed north there were, of course, boxcars, tracks and the station to contend with if he were forced to land.

No — it was quite clear to Willard: he'd have to get out of town for his trial flight.

He had that figured out already too. I was all ears.

"On Saddy mornin' we'll . . ."

"On Saturday morning I've got to go to Reverend Kreuz's for Bible School," I interrupted, but I wasn't looking for an excuse to back out.

"Well, then, we'll get up real early so's we can do it before Bible School, Wally . . . We'll knock down the glider here and we'll load the two wings on the fuselage . . ."

Willard was talking like a man inspired.

". . . and I can grab the tail for a handle, and with the buggy wheel out on front, it'll be just like pushin' a wheelbarrow . . ."

Willard was radiant, his eyes sparkling at the idea. He obviously hadn't realized until that very instant how well he had planned by putting that baby-buggy wheel out front!

"We'll cross the tracks, take the trail north past Scott McEachern's down into the valley. We'll use our sleighing hill, the steep one going down to the river. You can carry the tools, Wally!"

I was up bright and early the next morning. Willard was up even earlier and impatiently waiting for me. There was no holding him back. The farther out on the trail we went and the closer we came to the appointed hill, the faster he pushed his improvised barrow, breaking wind every now and again like a dray team pulling a heavy load. Had that happened at recess at school, he would have seized the opportunity to say, "Lick a' muzzle an' I fire again." But today he didn't have time for such levity. When we arrived at the proper spot, he lowered his burden to the ground and without even a minute's rest, aimed the fuselage straight down the slope, the lone baby carriage wheel propped up against a stone to keep it from rolling on downhill. Thereafter, the stillness was only broken by Willard's orders, like a surgeon's in an operating room.

"Hammer," he said tersely as he lifted one of the wings from the back of the fuselage to fit into the slot.

I handed him the hammer.

"Nails," was the next perfunctory command when he was sure the wing was properly fitted and balanced.

I handed him the nails . . . And so on for the second wing, then, grabbing an eight-pound ball of binder twine, he tied the loose end to the front end of the plane and told me to take it downhill, letting out twine as I went.

"What the deuce for?" I asked, for had he as much as uttered the word "twine" back in the garage?

"Just in case, Wally. If you see I want to come for a landing and mebbe can't negotiate it, you can help pull me in!"

Willard was worrying how he was going to get down out of the clouds when he hadn't even *one* foot off the ground! He was dead serious.

As I went down the slope I glanced back at Willard standing in the cockpit, his feet on the ground, holding the plane with a hand on each side, ready to lift the tail off the ground; the wheel at the front was still braced against the rock. It was a bedraggled *Albatross* by now, looking like nothing on earth — the rough mile-long ride out over the stony trail and pasture had taken its toll, the sacking and paper cover had loosened and was flapping in the slight breeze, and fluttering even more when Willard jockeyed his feet for a better position. I went still further downhill, feeding out more twine, gingerly making my way since the angle was all of forty-five degrees.

How, I wondered, could Willard, unencumbered, *run* down such an incline without falling, let alone now, saddled with fifty or sixty pounds of one-by-twos, sacking, packing crates and wrapping paper draped around him?

I stopped at the edge of the river bank. There was a full eight-foot drop into the water below. In the winter when we sped down that snowy slope we headed our sleighs for the old trail to the right, going on down to the ice of the frozen-over river, continuing along as long as we had any momentum. Only the daredevils would shoot straight down the hill and over the bank where I was standing, on to the snow-covered ice below. That path was Willard's objective now . . . I looked up at him. He had moved his *Albatross* so the front wheel was clear of the rock. I saw the tail lift from the ground. Willard, intently alert, deadly serious, was ready to "take off." If he was waiting for a signal from me, I improvised one, God only knows from where.

"Contact?"

"Contact," from Willard up on the hill.

"Whirl!"

With a lunge Willard set out. He wasn't letting the front wheel run on the ground as I assumed he would to relieve himself of part of the weight — he was carrying the entire craft himself!

Like a man getting unexpected strength from his adrenalins Willard broke into a gallop. More by good luck than good management he didn't stumble, for the forepart of his plane obstructed the view directly in front of him. On he charged, straight at me, gaining speed with every step. The contagion of his optimism suddenly suffused me with a thrill. Perhaps I was watching a miracle in the making. Maybe he *was* right, maybe he'd get his machine off the ground after all!

About ten feet from me Willard stumbled and, in saving himself from a fall, catapulted himself a foot or two into the air. When he normally would have touched ground again, he was over the edge of the river bank and, seconds later, in the river itself where he landed with an almost noiseless plop. Moments afterwards he surfaced, stuck his head up through the "cock pit" of the *Albatross,* shook hair and water out of his eyes like a water spaniel, gasped and spluttered.

"Did — you — see — me — fly?"

If being off the ground for three or four seconds — including those precious two it took to *fall* into the water — meant being airborne, then, I suppose, I had indeed seen Willard fly.

"Yes," I said, pulling in the twine hand over hand, drawing Willard and the *Albatross* towards shore, he still spluttering and gasping as he clutched at the wreckage which he appeared to be wearing around his neck like a grotesque Hawaiian lei.

"Leave 'er go, Wally," he said, and after getting his breath once more he added, "Don't bother pullin' 'er in, we can't save nothin'."

It was then I noticed that the *Albatross* was slowly sinking.

Like a man getting out of a manhole, Willard freed himself from the wreckage, dog-paddled towards the old fording trail where he could clamber up the bank. If indeed the wood in the glider could and, for a time, did float, the yards of wrapping paper and the gunny sacking were now waterlogged through and drawing the *Albatross* under.

Up on the bank beside me Willard stripped to the skin, wrung out his overalls and shirt before putting them back on. The *Albatross* was still perfectly visible although an inch or two below the surface of the water some twenty yards away now as the current slowly carried it downstream.

Reality generally put an end to my dreams. Willard, on the other hand, was neither downcast nor crestfallen at the sight of his dreamship — how many hours of work did it represent? — drawing away with the current. On the contrary: His achievement was exactly on a level with that of Orville and Wilbur Wright on December 17, 1903, or with that of Charles Lindberg in May, 1927, two years before when, "unknown and unsung" as the popular song of the day put it, he crossed the Atlantic in his *Spirit of Saint Louis*.

On the way home Willard, jubilant, was reliving that dramatic four-second flight. About halfway his brow furrowed but after only a minute his face brightened again.

"Know what, Wally?"

"No — what?"

"Next plane I'm going to build'll be a two seater!"

"A two-seater?"

"Yuh, an' you know what, Wally?"

"No — what?"

"I'll let *you* be first my first passenger!"

ECONOMICS

THERE was a big pail of freshly mixed gopher poison in Dad's "bug"; alongside it was an empty ten-pound syrup pail for me, and a couple of old long-handled blue-enameled ladling spoons. And Dad's twenty-two, of course. We were going to go out to the farm for a few hours to shoot and poison gophers. My interest was the three cents bounty I could collect for each gopher tail we turned in to the teacher. I really thought at the time that the municipality was *buying* these tails, that they had a commercial value just like ermine tails on the King's Coronation cloak. It never occurred to me at my age, that these pests could destroy enough grain to make them economically important.

We parked the "bug" on Dad's favorite knoll; he filled my little syrup pail with the still-dripping, poison-soaked grain and we set off. Dad showed me how to put a spoonful out — all I had to do was watch for the fresh holes of which there were dozens that spring. Every so often we would set down our pails and spend a few minutes shooting with the twenty-two.

I had two lessons that day, one in shooting, the other in economics. Dad never passed up a chance to get in practical instruction of this kind. Of course I wasn't always in a mood to listen — particularly if it meant I couldn't do something I had been planning on doing. I had a few fresh gopher tails in my pocket to account for a few lucky shots and I was already multiplying by three to figure out my bonanza when Dad pointed out how much a box of these twenty-two shots cost, how many of them there were in a box, and how many shots I had fired without a tail to show for them . . .

It was time to go home. I hadn't forgotten the strapping I had received in school from Mr. Mitchell some weeks before, nor the second licking, from Dad in the shop. I didn't ever expect that incident to be mentioned again because Dad didn't usually rehash unpleasant matters. I was thus a bit ashamed and embarrassed when the subject came up on the way home. Had Dad had second thoughts about my licking that day?

"What the Sam Hill were you doing in school anyway that made Mr. Mitchell give you such a trashing?"

It was most unusual to hear Dad use such an expression as "Sam Hill" and I detected a tone of the indignation in his voice which prompted its use then. I couldn't reply right away to his question either — it was already so far in the past that I had forgotten what I had been doing.

"I was trying to look back at Christina Blaine."

"Don't you see enough of Christina Blaine at recess without having to turn around in school when you're supposed to be doing your work?"

"Well," I said, "Jack Fender told us kids that red-headed girls even had red hair on their *gomisses* and I turned around to try to see on Christina if it was true. She's the only red-headed girl in our room."

"On their what?" Pa asked.

Heavens — didn't Dad know *anything?*

"On their *gomisses,* you know — between their legs! That's what Jack Fender calls it."

"Calls what . . .? When did Jack Fender ever mention such rubbish in front of you school kids?" gasped my father incredulously.

If Dad only knew *half* the things Jack Fender talked to us about . . . Why I learned more from him that year than I did from Mr. Mitchell!

A few seconds later, I'm sure without thinking, Dad asked: "Well, does she?"

It was really only when Dad uttered this question, one he certainly didn't intend to, one that he hardly expected me to answer, that I realized I had received both these lickings for nothing. Jack Fender's statements about red-headed girls' nether anatomy *still* had to be proven . . .

THE CALDWELLS
(continued)

ONLY Mr. Caldwell's pestering brought my Dad out to his farm again. All Frank had wanted the first time was to talk, and I had overheard most of their conversation. Dad liked to socialize too but that was for after working hours. Dad didn't care to gossip, however — it had perturbed him to hear what Mr. Caldwell said about his wife. No — Dad had just too many other things to do, his days were never long enough for his own pursuits without making unnecessary trips out to the country.

We hopped into the "bug" and were once more on our way. Of course Dad took along the twenty-two just in case we should see a gopher. Since it was only June it was quite a bit too early to take along the shotgun in case he saw a "chicken."

Dad unofficially began the duck, prairie chicken and Hungarian partridge shooting season a good month before it was legally open, and to average it out, to maintain some kind of equilibrium, he hunted for a month after it closed, fully aware that he was setting a bad example for his sons when he broke the law in this manner. He would be at a loss for an answer when I or Kalle would slyly ask if the hunting season had opened a month earlier than usual. He'd just clear his throat, move his toothpick over to the other side of his mouth and look straight ahead or off to one side as if he hadn't heard. He didn't even bother justifying himself, like some farmers, by saying that since he had been feeding these birds all year, he should get first (and, in Dad's case, last) crack at them before the city hunters came.

Angèle summed it up perfectly, since she bore the brunt of cleaning the game, saying that "hunting is just stronger than he is." Evidently she was translating one more of her French expressions. She also used to add, wrinkling her nose, that if Dad had to clean the birds himself, he wouldn't bring so many home.

Of course we stopped by our farm to see how our own crop was doing; the old Fordson was parked under the tree just as it had been the last time we went out to the Caldwells'. Just dropping in to see how the crop was, or for a five-minute stroll in the field of wheat, would put a smile on Dad's face for the rest of the day. We took a little turn by the corner where Dad was going to build the day he closed up the shop in town for good; we went over to the future orchard to see how the rows of fruit trees he had planted were progressing. They were still only inches high with the wooden identification tags from the nursery firmly attached — but my Dad could already see them feet high and heavy with fruit. In short, we dawdled unnecessarily.

Dad regarded this trip as a duty. As Caldwell's oldest and perhaps only close friend, he felt he should go out and hear his tale of woe once more, although there was nothing he could do to help. But my father was loath to hear anyone speak ill of another person, and particularly to hear a man speak ill of his wife as Mr. Caldwell had done the last time.

We were both surprised when we turned into the Caldwells' yard. Mr. Caldwell was a changed person. He had thrown the weight of ten years' worry from his shoulders, having acquired an absorbing new interest in life. Indeed it was on account of this new interest that he had called my father out to see him.

Mrs. Caldwell was a Leader, but was frustrated that her God-given talents were so limited in scope in Minby, being virtually unknown beyond the tiny circle of her church. Her firm conviction that she was destined for far finer things prompted her to undertake that first public church meeting and picnic some years before, which had been a regular feature ever since. The first year it had been a very *intimate* group, consisting of the regular church members plus a few of these members' invited guests. Instead of meeting in the church that Sunday — it would have been too small for the purpose — Mrs. Caldwell insisted they come out to *her* place. The Reverend Hobbs preached his sermon outside, they ate their picnic lunches, they rejoiced in the good weather the Heavenly Father had given them and Mrs. Caldwell said: "We must do this again *next* year!" From such unpretentious beginnings an Acorn took seed.

The following year it was called "Worship in Nature" and the year after that the title changed, albeit slightly, to "Worship with Nature" and when Mrs. Caldwell heard someone commenting on her "wonderful service in the grove" that little phrase stuck and it was called the "Service in the Grove" ever afterwards. Didn't "Service in the Grove" have the same character and consonance as "Church in the Wildwood"?

Once the pattern was set, each succeeding year was bigger and better than the one before and Mrs. Caldwell started planning the following year's program the morning after the one just over. If the minister did the preaching, and if the rest of the women from the church brought the lunches, there was actually little left for Mrs. Caldwell to do except "have the responsibility of it" but it was tacitly admitted by all and sundry that without her leadership, without her talents for organization, her "Service in the Grove" would never have become the Mighty Oak it now was. Was there anything like it in Missenden or Culbertson? The answer was "No." After the second or third year it was widely publicized that the annual gathering was nondenominational. In short, Mrs. Caldwell's "Service in the Grove" was rivaling Jack Smythe's corn feed in the number of people attracted.

For the last few years now there had been at least one ball game and sometimes two, and that really brought the crowd! It was Reverend Shandy who had courageously put this idea into Mrs. Caldwell's head. *He* was the baseball fan; but he had been clever enough to lead up to it in such a manner as to make her think she had thought of it first.

Any amateur band too for forty miles around could be sure of being welcomed with open arms if they came and played. They were always given a free lunch and could count on two lines in the *The Missenden Thunderbolt* when Mrs. Caldwell sent in her *compte-rendu.*

The high point of the evening was the address of the officiating minister. Over the years Mrs. Caldwell had accumulated a few thousand board feet of lumber and sawhorses enough to have started up business if she had wanted to. There were two-by-eights and two-by-tens which could be used with the sawhorses to serve as tables upon which the women piled their lunches; the same two-by-tens served as temporary seats afterwards when the tables were dismantled and set up again as benches so the people could listen to the sermon in solid comfort.

What could she add this year?

Mr. Caldwell — yes, *Mr.* Caldwell had come up with the answer!

It must have been as big a surprise to Mrs. Caldwell as it was to my Dad, but for different reasons. It was a still bigger surprise and a very pleasant one for Dad to hear that the husband and wife were again speaking to one another.

Of course I remembered our last trip out and Mr. Caldwell's threats as he unburdened himself to my father. What a change in the man now — I had never seen him so excited as he was today. It hadn't taken much to convince his wife that what they really needed was a platform, a real platform from which the minister could deliver his inspiring address, a platform from which a band could give a little afternoon concert, a platform big enough for a few guests of honor as a fitting background to the minister as he preached. No doubt Mrs. Caldwell could see herself in the most prominent seat, the minister at *her* right . . .; a platform with a canvas roof, sidewalls, and curtains that could be parted, for shade from the sun if it were an afternoon service, or shelter from the rain if a shower should come up; in short, a platform the likes of which had never been seen around Minby, a platform from which something *dramatic,* some *surprise* could be prepared . . .

Mr. Caldwell spoke his wife's own language when he injected the words "dramatic" and "surprise." Hadn't Mrs. Caldwell made it a point of honor to come forth each year with a new surprise? That was enough for her to loosen the purse strings, since it appeared to be she who was chancellor of the Caldwell exchequer. And really it wasn't such a bad investment after all, for couldn't the platform be used year after year thereafter?

"What's my job in all this?" asked my Dad.

In his eagerness to explain, Mr. Caldwell at a half-run was leading my father by the hand much as he would a small boy over to his big machine shed where we had been the time before. In a twinkling Dad saw that he was to do the iron work. He would have to make braces for the platform corners, six long threaded diagonal rods each several yards long, two long enough to support the structure at ground level, two more at the platform level immediately under the flooring, the third pair about eight or nine feet above the floor.

"Why on earth do you want it so high?" asked Pa incredulously, "it'll be as big as the CPR water tower in Missenden! You know, you've got enough two-by-eights to build a small elevator. Have you no idea what all this is going to cost?''

"Oh," said Mr. Caldwell, "the wife's always been wanting to give surprises and she'll pay for it. She'll pay for the one I'm going to give her this year too." He chuckled and with a wink at Pa as if my Dad also knew what deviltry he was up to, he gave himself a hearty slap on the knee to punctuate his statement, "Besides, she's got piles of money . . .''

Dad, I'm afraid, didn't catch on. I knew *for sure* just hearing Mr. Caldwell talk, that what he had in mind *still* had something to do with what he had been talking about when we were out the time before.

"But what's all the hurry, Mr. Caldwell; couldn't this have waited another month, six weeks . . .? This is only June. Your wife doesn't usually have her meeting so early in the year!''

"You know me, Ingve, when I get an idea into my head, nothing will stop me. I just want to get the platform up *my* way and make sure it's all right in lots of time. Can I pick up the rods next week?''

Dad told him that that was really rushing things; he assured him nevertheless that he could. Mr. Caldwell said that his wife would pay for it, and sure enough this time as we headed for the "bug" she met us in the lane. I seldom saw her up close. She twisted her face into the grimace that was accepted as her smile. She had her check book in one hand and her pen in the other ready. The check was already made out to my Dad, filled out in every detail except for the amount.

As we drove home, Dad, blissfully ignorant of his part in the unfolding drama, was in a cheerful frame of mind. Mr. Caldwell's unaccustomed good humor and Mrs. Caldwell's grimace were enough to convince him that there had really been an armistice and that they had agreed to agree for a change.

"What day is today?" Dad asked.

"Saturday."

"I mean what date?"

"The eighth."

"We'll have to remember to come out to the picnic!"

"When'll that be?" I asked.

"Oh, in six, seven weeks, I expect."

GRADE EIGHT "ENTRANCE" EXAMS

ALLOW GRADE SEVEN to write the "Entrance" Exams? Dad said he had never heard anything so preposterous before. Of course he didn't say this when we kids were around. That would have been tantamount to saying Mr. Mitchell was crazy. That approached Dad's opinion of my teacher that year. His precept, however, drilled in to us so many times in the past was as follows: If you can't say anything good or anything nice about someone, then don't open your mouth at all. Curtailing conversation this way was a constant source of irritation to my mother because, as it so often happened, it was usually the bits of news that weren't quite so nice that she liked best to hear. Angèle, of course, had relayed my Dad's statement to me. After all, I was involved.

I was only one of a dozen affected by what Dad considered Mr. Mitchell's "plumb foolish" decision which was as follows: The Grade Seven students would write the Entrance Examinations along with the Grade Eight. What he said, in justification of this statement, was absolutely true with certain qualifications, to wit: Since Grade Seven and Grade Eight had been taking the same work all year, then the Grade Seven students had as good a chance of passing as those in Grade Eight.

Indeed, we had had exactly the same work all year. More specifically, we had *all* done next to nothing. Yet Mr. Mitchell must have been convinced he had done a good job of teaching and that we in Grade Seven really and truly had as good a chance of passing into Grade Nine as did the Grade Eighters. Would he have let us write otherwise?

Dad was flabbergasted. He raised his cap, scratched his head, moved his toothpick from one side to the other in his mouth.

Dad was skeptical about skipping grades. When I had been moved ahead in the past he had always gone to see the teacher to ask if it was really the wise thing to do. This year he had been worried and troubled as he watched our lack of progress all year, our lack of homework assignments, and still worse, our obvious lack of interest in anything pertaining to school. He had heard the rumors too, all of them true, alas, of Mr. Mitchell's inefficiency as a teacher. Dad couldn't wait for the school year to end so the "Board" could see about a replacement.

Always, when we came home from school with our report cards, Dad would examine them critically, missing absolutely nothing before he signed them. No matter how good they were, we always "could of done better" — that was his formula and it never varied from one month to the next, nor from one of his kids to the next. For us, when we were in school, all we had to do from nine until three thirty was to "pay 'tention" and do our work. Wasn't that the sole reason we were in school? Was there any reason why we shouldn't *all* come home *all* the time with hundred's in *all* our subjects?

I was in Grade Seven. I interpreted Mr. Mitchell's announcement that we would write Grade Eight Entrance Examinations as follows: No teacher in his right mind would take such a decision upon himself unless he was sure a good number would pass. In spite of the very evidence against it, I concluded optimistically, that since some of us *might* pass, *I* might even be among the elect. Had I ever failed? Hadn't I been pushed on twice before?

I hopefully went through my scribblers looking for notes that weren't there. I belatedly attacked my school texts nine months behind time, reading chapter after chapter that I should have read months before. A stupid feeling of hope had shot through both grades, as a matter of fact, the majority of the pupils reasoning as I did. It would cost us two dollars to write, of course, but we in Grade Seven, even if we failed the Entrance Exams, would be going on to Grade Eight anyway. I had everything to win — what, in short, could I lose? I was sure I would be taking Grade Eight next year and, *with a lucky fluke,* maybe Grade Nine.

Only one or two had written Entrance Examinations before, so almost all of us were unfamiliar with the procedure — we had to be briefed. We were about thirty, including a sprinkling of kids from the country schools who had taken part of Grade Eight by correspondence.

There was an air of quiet seriousness that first morning too as we took our seats for exam number one. Even one of the members of the school board was attracted by the solemnity of the occasion — or did regulations demand his presence that first day? No less a person than Hedley Cantelon himself, chairman of the Minby school board, was sitting imposingly at the back of the room, arms crossed, his benignly stupid smile spread across his face like a big capital "V." Two of his boys were writing. Of course they would both be taking Nine next year and he was no doubt giving up silent thanks for having had a teacher like Mr. Mitchell who had made this possible.

Examination foolscap — how appropriately some things are named! — had been passed out beforehand to each desk. We all came gravely in and soberly took our seats; after a few minutes the examination questions themselves were removed from a sealed envelope as we looked anxiously on. This was the examination in Mathematics. Two and a half dozen pairs of startled eyes were soon studying the questions.

No one had a chance. Certainly none of Mr. Mitchell's pupils did. I knew I couldn't pass it, and in spite of a violent desire to put up my hand to leave the room, I took up writing equipment and ignoring the seething turmoil in my guts, tried the first question. The odd question that could be done with a good knowledge of Grade Six and a little ingenuity I could and did do. I exercised my brain more in that two-hour tussle than I had all year. The geometry part I couldn't do at all because I had never had a geometry text. Geometry hadn't even been prescribed for Grade Seven, and I had only seen Mr. Mitchell teach one or two lessons in this subject to Grade Eight. When the bell came I nevertheless thought that I might have gotten half the questions right. Then followed the farce of putting my paper in a special envelope, sealing it, writing my name on another long narrow strip of paper which I stuck to the big envelope containing my Exam paper. So much ritual, so many precautions for what?

The next day we were examined in Literature and Composition. It was a foregone conclusion once I saw the Literature questions that I was again wasting my time. I did what I could on the Composition part, was done with an hour left over but too proud to turn in my paper. Several had already handed in theirs. I was done in half time for the simple reason that we had had so little instruction in grammar that we weren't even familiar with the working vocabulary; we didn't know what some of the *words* meant with which the questions were phrased! The same smart students who had turned in their papers early that day before were having their joke and smiling again today, only halfheartedly however, probably more to reassure themselves. I glanced around the room and could see on most faces — since it had taken them no longer than me to pour out their scant knowledge — "You hand yours in and I'll hand in mine."

With a few minutes to go a knock came at the door. It was one of the Gottselig boys, Theresa's older brother, who had come to tell her that their mother had dropped dead from a heart attack only an hour before. It was a shock to Theresa, who left the room in tears, and an awful shock to me too — I had been talking to Mrs. Gottselig on my eleventh birthday only a month before. Theresa never came back to finish, nor did she return to school in the fall. She stayed home to help her older sister Magdalena look after the family. She could always brag that she had never failed a grade the whole time she was in school, *not even that awful year* when we had Mr. Mitchell as a teacher.

I, too was mercifully saved from the farce of writing the rest of the examinations. The morning of the third day when I awoke, I had something in addition to my usual itchy eczema to bother me. When I showed it to Mom at breakfast she sent me flying upstairs again with a "Get back into bed, kid!" She was sure I had the measles.

When I lightly hopped back under the covers I jubilantly kicked my heels in the air, happy to give expression to the satisfaction and relief I felt. I was fit as a fiddle, positively wonderful. When had I felt better? *And no more of these damned exams!* When I heard the school bell summoning the others, I felt much like Mr. Séguin's goat must have felt high up in the mountains when she heard the bell calling her back to the farm below . . . With its last peal dying away, a profound feeling of relief swept over me. I had been saved!

About ten minutes later I heard steps and a strange voice coming up the stairs with my mother. It was Dr. Grenz. "Uncle" Martin, the truant officer, had spotted the doctor driving through Minby minutes after Dad informed him I probably had the measles. Since I was writing the all-important Entrance Examinations, a serious check had to be made before I was allowed not to write. In less than a minute Dr. Grenz had thrown back the blankets and was viewing the other parts of my body not marked by eczema. He confirmed Mom's provisional diagnosis.

"Measles all right. Put him in a room by himself, keep him out of the sun, and in quarantine for ten days!"

Quarantine? I had only vaguely heard that word before and then with regard to others. Would I really have to stay in bed all that time? Hell's bloody bells! — in less than a week our holidays were going to start!

This put an entirely different light on the subject. I didn't want to write the rest of the exams. But then I didn't want to be sick for a single day of our holiday either, damn it, there had to be some mistake.

"And he was writing his Entrance . . ." Mom said, faking a long face, introducing an unconvincing note of tragedy in her voice, for she was under no delusion whatever about her boys' chances at passing. She was certainly wishing at that very moment that Kalle was sick in bed beside me so he wouldn't have to finish writing either.

"Oh, there's no reason why he can't go ahead and write them at home," said Doctor Grenz expansively. There was no mistaking the genuineness of the cheerful ring in this good-humor-man's voice. I wanted to throttle him as he continued: "I'll give you a little note for the teacher. This sort of thing happens every year, you know."

As the two went downstairs again I concluded I didn't feel so good after all: I'd be staying home, sure, but I'd still have to write the damned exams! This wasn't the way I thought it was going to be a scant twenty minutes before, and I was astonished at the fickleness of fate.

True to his word, Dr. Grenz saw both Mr. Mitchell and Mr. Cantelon, the chairman. It was officially confirmed that I had the measles and that I'd have to stay at home. But I would be permitted to write! Before the morning was much older I heard more voices downstairs. A few minutes later I was propped up in bed, pen in one hand, studying the Grade Eight History paper. It might just as well have been a tablet of cuneiform inscriptions that I was to decipher, or the Rosetta Stone — one would have made just as much sense to me as the other.

What caused my sudden headache? the sight of the paper? or the sickness finally asserting itself? My head swam as I looked at these absolutely incomprehensible questions. I finished the two or three I felt I could tackle, sealed my answer paper and with it my fate in the big envelope and pulled the blankets over my head.

I had no appetite for lunch . . .

When I saw the exam for the afternoon, I threw up what little food I had managed to get down only half an hour before. I broke out in a cold sweat after reading through the questions. I couldn't do a single one and I knew it. This time I was really sick, unmistakably and seriously ill.

And so passed my first experience with the Departmental Entrance Examinations. Had Kalle and I been in a class like Mr. Ewer's in Melfort the year before when 29 out of 29 wrote and got through, 13 with Honors, we might have passed too.

I had another chance the next year.

SUMMER HOLYDAYS

AND SO BEGAN the longest, dullest, bleakest six weeks of my existence, duller, bleaker and more monotonous even than the concentrated six weeks of Bible School the previous summer with Reverend Alvar in the Old Stone School. I was glad that I had fallen sick with the measles before school was over since it had spared me the shame of writing most of the Grade Eight Entrance Examinations. However, once the novelty of being a patient had worn off (the second day) it was hard to pass the time. My younger brothers and sister contracted measles too, Mom had seen to that, and we were confined to the house. Greta and Kalle, both older than I, had had the malady the *last* time it had been around, before I was born. Mom had the theory prevalent in Minby at the time — perhaps it still is — that kids, all kids *had* to have measles and certain other childhood sicknesses, since they could be far more serious if contracted later on. The doctor had also warned that too much light was hard on the eyes. Since I had started wearing glasses the first year in school, Mom took Dr. Grenz's warning particularly to heart and I lived in a twilight world for days on end because of his injunction. Not being allowed to read for pastime was bad; to be penned up inside in the nicest possible weather with the other Minby kids noisily spending their holidays outside, oftentimes in our own back yard, a supplice.

Yet my quarantine didn't bother me as much as it could have. I had very vivid and painful recollections of Bible School the year before but when it was over it was over! I knew now, on the contrary — although

I hadn't known the first couple of days of the measles, that as soon as my present incarceration was finished, Reverend Kreuz was going to take our confirmation class, all boys, to the lake "for instruction." Normally to go to the lake was about the biggest picnic Dad could offer us, only surpassed in magnitude by our annual trip to the Exhibition. Going to the lake was actually a rare treat since it was a long way away; the only good fishing lake, as a matter of fact, was forty-five miles from Minby, half of them over prairie trails, the last two miles through pasture with no road at all. To drive there and back on a Sunday, and to spend a profitable time fishing was quite an undertaking and took the whole day.

My quarantine fell in the latter part of June and the first week of July. July 1, always a big day for Minby or Missenden, might just as well have been any ordinary Monday that year. There were Sports Days all around us, but the Viggos might just as well have been off in Timbuktu. Thursday, July 4, came and went, and with it the other Sports Days that hadn't been held on the first. And what attractions! The House of Davids team played at Rottingdean only fifteen miles away on July the First, and the Texas Colored Giants at Griswold on the Fourth, and we at home, had missed both these spectacular events.

What hot and long, endless, empty days! One exciting event took place so quickly that it was not until later that we realized its full impact on the Viggo household. We — that is those with the measles — were confined to the parlor. That was our part of the house during our period of quarantine — there we had to stay; but the last day was up on the morrow, Sunday. This Saturday afternoon we were playing fitfully at checkers and cards when the screen door of the verandah flew open and just as quickly slammed shut again. It was Gene Dempsey, Angèle's tempestuous suitor, in from his farm. He had finally given up his garage as a bad job. He came to our place very seldom at this time of day, but when he did, his penetrating voice could be heard all over.

"Hurry up. Angèle, we've just got half an hour to make it!"

"Make it? Make what, Gene?"

"The train!"

"The train? What train? Where to? What for?" asked Angèle, her questions piling up and becoming louder and louder as she emerged from the depths of the pantry.

"To the city — we're going to get married!"

And that, verbatim, is exactly how Gene Dempsey proposed and swept our Angèle off her feet. She submitted to his half-hour ultimatum that Saturday afternoon like she submitted to all his ultimatums thereafter. Had they discussed marriage before? It's doubtful — wouldn't Angèle have said something about it to Mom? She must have known her association with Gene would one day result in marriage and undoubtedly encouraged him. She couldn't have expected that it would end in a double-quick ceremony like this, without all the fancy trimmings, for Angèle was just the kind to want all the extras. When anyone around Minby sneaked off and got married like that, wasn't it because they had to? Gene and Angèle took the train, they "got spliced," but I didn't notice the changes brought about by Angèle's sudden departure for several weeks to come, mostly because of the upheaval and change of routine occasioned by our departure for the lake and catechism. Angèle was at home when I left — she wasn't there when I returned.

Reverend Kreuz had outlined what each family was to send with their kids to avoid useless duplication. We first went to Müllers' Hotel to pick up Ron. In spite of the explicit instructions she had received, Mrs. Müller had still packed twice as much equipment and provisions for "her" Ronnie as Kalle and I had between us. Luckily

. . . And thence to Haugens to pick up Erik with his miserable little suitcase. Reverend Kreuz, following behind in the Model T, had "Alkali" Willie and Willie's scintillating conversation, and one of the other boys for company. The others followed with their parents.

We didn't set up camp down by the beach in the trees as we could have done. Instead, we pitched our tents on the edge of the prairie, the very edge where it started to slope down to the lake shore below. From our point of vantage we could look north, east or south and swear we were on the bald prairies a mile out of Minby. It was only when we faced west and looked downhill that we could see the cool inviting surface of the water beckoning below.

After freezing the first nights — Ronnie Müller from the hotel was the only one who, thanks to the foresight of his mother, had a mattress along — we were up with the birds and learned catechism, Bible verses, followed by more catechism and more Bible verses. It was much like being fed a diet of boiled, unsalted potatoes for our three meals followed by more boiled, unsalted potatoes the next day and the next. Every morning we said grace before breakfast and had a little chapel service immediately after, during which we sang a few verses of the hymn for the day. Without any musical accompaniment, and perhaps just because most boys don't like to sing anyway, we weren't carried away in our enthusiasm. It was a grim performance; but since "Worship through Music" (the hymn) was down as part of our daily program it was continued the whole six weeks we were there. Reverend Kreuz admonished us every morning "to sing up" and berated us when we didn't; he complimented us a few times even when it wasn't any better, hoping, perhaps, that his pious little fib might inspire us to do a better job on the morrow. Why these chapel services at all when our whole day was taken up with "the Word" as it was?

It was Reverend Kreuz's hope that we accomplish as much in a day as we had previously done each Saturday in Minby during the public school year. Theoretically that would have been possible in the amount of time at our disposal, since we weren't going to regular school and had little else to do but our few cooking tasks. But isn't there a tremendous difference in doing one assignment of memory work by repetition over seven days, and in trying to do the equivalent amount of work in a day? . . . followed by a similar massive dose the next, each new assignment more monotonous and stultifying than the preceding one? It seemed tacitly agreed by all, Reverend Kreuz too, of course, that "Horseface" Schurk, poor little "Alkali" Willie, the prize blister of Minby Public School, should be exempted from every onerous camp task, since he required all his time to study. Though Willie boasted the honest German name of Schurk, he led the life of Reilly the whole six weeks at the lake. It seemed just as tacitly understood that he was the only one never expected to know his lines when everyone else had to know theirs or catch hell if they didn't. I had the naive idea that Reverend Kreuz had been too softhearted to tell Willie's parents that their son wasn't bright enough to keep up with the rest of us, and that he would begin again with the new class in the fall. Why else would "Horseface" Schurk have been singled out for Special Privileges? I wouldn't have believed the truth if I had been told then . . . I found it incredible when I did learn it many years later.

We were intrigued by another camp, identical in size to ours, about four hundred yards distant from our own. It also consisted of a group of boys of our age. But since, as we soon found out, they were Catholics under the protective eye of the Priest, we might as well have been at the North Pole, they at the South. There had been, to my knowledge, no contact between the two camp leaders, yet *some* means of communication had been established, probably on a *spiritual* level; and the essence of it was that Protestantism in its purest form, and Catholicism in its, shouldn't mix, especially when it was being distilled and catechized in two places in so unadulterated a form. Between these two Christian fronts a no man's land materialized that first day between the Saxons on the hill and the Romans down below, and it remained the whole time we were out. There was this difference, however: they *had fun,* they went swimming and fishing, regularly, they fished *every* day, not just the "fish" days.

Busy as Dad was, he found time to come out a few times after supper to bring along fresh supplies and check how we were getting along. It was a six-hour, ninety-mile return trip each time over roads that were neither familiar nor good. On his first trip, thanks to a long distance S.O.S. from the minister, he brought out mattresses; he brought out newspapers, he brought Reverend Kreuz his mail which he read very importantly the next day. One newspaper article had a ghoulish fascination for me. It gave all the details: "Saskatchewan murderer pays for crime with his life. . . . Quickly Hangman Ellis placed the prisoner in the centre of the platform in the dazzling light of the high-powered electric lamps, bound the ankles, adjusted the black cap on the head, calling to Reverend Alcock to commence the Lord's Prayer. The clergyman commenced the Anglican form of the prayer, Megill answering distinctly from the muffled folds of the black cap. As he replied 'Deliver us from evil,' the trap was sprung. Quietly the doors swung open, and the murderer had given his life. Death was instantaneous."

I couldn't sleep that night or the next. Each day thereafter when we recited the Lord's Prayer I maintained an uneasy silence at the "Deliver us from evil . . ." and thought about those "muffled folds of the black cap."

It amazed me how Reverend Kreuz could get so many letters, so many periodicals, more pulp, in fact, than our whole family used to get back in Minby. I was at an age when I didn't know there was such a thing as Fourth Class Mail. Once Dad said a bit wistfully that he would be out again the following Friday evening, commenting how nice it would be to take back a fresh fish or two to Minby . . . But even that hint didn't move Reverend Kreuz to give us a half day off. First things first, no doubt. It wasn't that we didn't have tackle — Mrs. Müller sent along enough with Ronnie to do the gang of us.

Reverend Kreuz's immediate pursuit each time after Dad's departure, was a minute examination of the baskets and jars of provisions sent along by the mothers. It is true there may have been some perishables among them. We were sitting around one of the two tables we used, one of the kind with the benches solidly nailed to the table itself. This particular table happened to be on the very edge of the top of the crest and sloping slightly. Reverend Kreuz, his back to the lake (as usual) was sitting on the low side, the freshly unpacked food spread out temptingly in front of him. The two benches of this table had been quite full, a couple of us kids on each side. As we got up one at a time the equilibrium had been maintained. When I got up, however, the last one on the side opposite the pastor — which would indicate my position in the gourmet hierarchy — the table overbalanced, toppling backwards, overturning completely, landing on top of Reverend Kreuz in the bushes a few yards below the crest. I had long known there were times when to laugh was inappropriate. I learned that evening that there were times when a sympathetic smile even when accompanied by a helping hand was out of place . . .

Another time when Dad drove out — it was the last of July — in addition to the usual food, newspapers and letters he had for Reverend Kreuz, he had two identical letters. One was for Kalle, the other for me.

These were the results of the Grade Eight Entrance Examinations sent out by the Department of Education. Ordinarily, if Dad had thought these missives bore tidings of great joy, he or Mom back in Minby would have opened and read them, telephoning us the good news without delay. Both Dad and Mom suspected the worst . . . Kalle had his open, the results noted, and had silently turned it over to Dad. Kalle had written all the subjects and hadn't passed a single one. I was jittery as I fumbled with mine, but finally I got it opened too. "History-28, Literature and Composition-32, Mathematics-68." They were the only three I had written. I had at least passed the Math, I thought, and with my finger under the "68" I handed it over to Dad without a word. I didn't want Kalle to know I had got a subject when he hadn't passed any.

Dad was just as tactful. Just as silently, he put his calloused forefinger under the "possible" mark in the adjacent column, which read 150, and soberly handed the sheet back to me. I would have needed 75 to have had a passing mark. For what reason had all the classes except Mathematics been marked out of 100? Had geometry been marked separately and given 50, with the other 100 for arithmetic? Like Kalle I hadn't passed any of my subjects either. But then I didn't really give a damn. Hadn't Mr. Mitchell said that we in Grade Seven would be going into Grade Eight anyway?

These examination results were a terrible blow for Kalle. Now he knew for sure he would be spending the next year in the same grade, and that I, his younger brother, would be in it with him. It was a catastrophe which resulted in a different relationship between us thereafter. Until that very instant the difference in age, his proficiency in athletics, his general all-around education and abilities, had given him a natural superiority over me. Wasn't he two years my senior? This was all liquidated in a matter of seconds. The Grade Eight results, published in the daily papers of August 6 for the whole province to see, confirmed that there hadn't been one successful candidate from Minby. Bad as these catastrophic results had been, we still did not know that matters could be even worse. We still hadn't heard, nor were we to know for a few more weeks, that the School Board, incredible as this may sound, had hired Mr. Mitchell to come back in the fall!

And so our "holiday" at the Lake was coming to an end . . . The final week was the next thing to hell on earth since, with Dad's last batch of newspapers there was one whole special supplement devoted to the Provincial Exhibition. To have to read this while surfeited with catechism and Bible verses was like being in a hairshirt, even more so than during the quarantine for measles.

On Sunday my mind was wandering when it should have been on things spiritual. I was singularly inattentive at grace before breakfast and again at hymn time right after, for I knew that *perhaps at that precise moment* the Exhibition Trains would be thundering through Minby on their way to the city. I had seen them every year as far back as I could remember. Dad always took us kids down to the loading platform where we could watch them, and this would be the first year I had missed. The arrival of that train early Sunday morning each year brought a good many people to the village for that hectic minute or two to enjoy the spectacle as the two or three sections of the Special raced through Minby, whistling as they went. That was the closest the Kaschl kids ever got to an exhibition. This year I wouldn't see even that.

On Monday I said to myself, "Today is nickel day"

— the day Dad always chose to be at the Exhibition, for with six children in tow, five cents for a ride instead of the usual dime was an appreciable saving. And how I wanted to see that "Wall of Death," and those motorcycles traveling around on that perpendicular wall at a hundred miles an hour!

On Tuesday I started thinking Dad *might* drive past the lake with the family and pick up Kalle and me and take us to the Exhibition *after all*. I admitted, of course, it would look rather unfair to the other boys in the class. I didn't believe in Heaven or Hell, but I still believed in miracles . . .

But Dad didn't come that day, nor did he come Wednesday, nor the day after, nor the day after that . . .

On Saturday night when I knew the fireworks were being blasted off, when the draws were being made for the lucky car-winners, the confirmation class was all under the covers, stretched out on our springless mattresses, spending our last night in camp. Tomorrow would be the special outdoor service to mark the final day; Reverend Kreuz had planned for it just like old lady Caldwell always planned for her "Service in the Grove." The entire congregation would all drive out to worship, pick up their kids, and take them back to Minby. There was to be a picnic. Yes — then we'd all go back to Minby. Tomorrow, Thank God, would be our last day at the lake.

Then Reverend Kreuz would be leaving on his hard-earned vacation.

Then *we* would have a few holidays too.

MOM TAKES HER TRIP

DAD HAD been to Sweden most of December and January. So when Mom got the letter from my *gudmor* (godmother) a while back, it was decided that she too was going to have a holiday. What Mrs. Rosenkvist wrote was very brief, to the point, and went like this:

"Dear Mrs. Viggo:

Don't you never get away from Minby? How about letting Ingve look after hisself for a few days? How about coming down to the city for a few weeks? Let's be sisters again and have fun like we did in the old days. Write right away that you're coming. My girls can look after the store.

Love,
Laura Rosenkvist"

Mom would be taking a trip! Mom, who had scarcely ever been alone outside of her home in Minby, was going to take the train all by herself to the city. It was incredible, simply unbelievable! Mom reminded us proudly, with an I-told-you-so toss of the head, and a "Didn't I, Ingve?" to our Dad for confirmation, that she had made the trip all alone from Sweden to the States so many years before.

"Yes," Mom said rather righteously the first few days, "don't you think *I* deserve a holiday too once in a while, like anybody else?"

Indeed Dad had been away almost two months; Greta, who had been away at college, had as good as had a holiday. And then Kalle and I had just had six weeks "out at the lake" for Bible instruction which Mom insisted had been a holiday, a statement I hotly contested each time I heard it.

Of course, since Mom didn't have "a thing to wear" and since she simply wasn't going to be seen "with that old rag of a coat" a special order went off to Eaton's for new clothes "for the trip."

"Why don't you just wait until you're in the city and go shopping with Mrs. Rosenkvist, she'll take you to all the Department Stores?" asked Dad.

The puzzled, uncomprehending look on Mom's face would make one believe that my Dad was suggesting she go clear to New York to some exclusive Fifth Avenue shop. Were there really *other* stores besides Eaton's and Simpson's where one could get a good coat?

Mom was tremendously enthusiastic about the trip when Mrs. Rosenkvist's letter first arrived; but a curious change seemed to come over her about ten days later after she had received her parcel from Eaton's, after she had tried on her new finery, after she had seen that everything fit. It seemed that she had already extracted all the enjoyment she was going to have from her trip.

With about a week to go, Mom said she would sooner be at home than "traipsing off to the city like a gypsy." Pa turned her own arguments against her: Didn't she deserve a holiday too? Hadn't *he* been to Europe for a couple of months? Did she really think we couldn't get along without her for a couple of weeks?

"A week will be enough!" Mom compromised hurriedly, her mind made up . . .

With three days to go, Mom seemed to take spirit again as if the trip wasn't going to be so bad after all; and hadn't Mrs. Rosenkvist written once more to reassure her that she and the girls would be there to meet her at the station?

Two days before the big day, Mom packed and repacked her two suitcases for the last time to see if she had remembered everything, and they were standing ready downstairs by the door, "for the trip." As if she was likely to leave them behind . . .

The evening before, she had carefully hung up her coat, the dress she was going to be wearing, her scarf, her gloves, her — as a matter of fact everything that she was going to put on "for the trip." And that last evening too, suddenly recalling that it was the thing to do no doubt, she sent me down to Kovacz's for a little five-cent bag of peppermints, the only kind of candy she ever ate. Mom, who didn't eat six pieces of candy a year, was going to have a little bag of peppermints with her "for the trip," this long two-hour journey to the city.

Came the forenoon of the last day. We were all sitting around the big table having our noon meal, it would be weeks before she would be dining with us again . . .

"One week!" corrected Mom.

We tried to cheer her up. By now even Dad seemed a bit melancholy. What was to have been a merry farewell dinner could have been a funeral service.

"You just want to get rid of me," Mom sniffed, looking for an excuse for us all to tell her to stay. I thought she was going to have a sentimental cry; and tears did come when we finally saw her off on the four o'clock train after school. We kids laughed a bit at her show of emotion.

"It's nothing to laugh about," said Dad, swallowing very soberly, a bit gruffly.

The house without Mom *wasn't* the same when we got back from the station. Elsa, my younger sister who had learned everything she knew about cooking from Mom, prepared just as appetizing an evening meal as my mother could have done, incorporating the leftovers from our noon meal, the very meal that Mom had cooked for us five short hours before. But it didn't taste the same. Nothing tasted the same.

Halfway through supper Dad asked what day it was.

Three-quarters of the way through the meal he asked when Mom said she would be back.

We all ate in silence.

At eight o'clock Dad was still looking at the headlines of the front page of the first newspaper, he who regularly read two and sometimes three each evening before retiring.

A few minutes before nine he turned on CFCN for his news, but he seemed to be listening for something else. When the news did come on a few minutes later, he was down in the basement putting coal in the furnace, a task which he never performed until going to bed.

At half-past nine when Elsa went out to warm up the coffee pot, Dad told her not to bother, he didn't care for any. Dad turn down a cup of coffee?

At ten o'clock all the lights were out in the house and everyone was in bed. Truly it was as if the end of the world had come.

At midnight I had to get up to go to the bathroom. I could hear my Dad rolling over in bed and sighing very audibly. Perhaps the midnight train had awakened him as it may have awakened me . . .

I wasn't back in bed more than five or ten minutes when I heard the muffled sound of the outside shed door downstairs being pulled shut. Dad was out of bed in seconds and downstairs unlocking the kitchen door. Mom was back! I could hear my father alternately scolding her for not staying, and laughing his pleasure at seeing her back home again.

"I just took one look at that bed," I heard Mom say in a complaining voice that was anything but convincing, "and I said to myself, If I have sleep in *that* then there'll be no sleep for me . . . And besides, Ingve, all I did was sit and look at myself, she was in and out of her store all the time, I might just as well have been back home here in Minby.''

I heard a clatter from the kitchen stove and a chunk of wood thrown in; a few minutes later I could hear the coffee pot as it started to perk, and in another minute although it was well after midnight there was the unmistakable odor of coffee percolating and the subdued mixed tones of two happy voices as I fell asleep.

I learned the next day that it was six o'clock in the morning before Mom and Dad finally went to bed. The things they had to talk about! Mom had been gone from Minby exactly eight hours and thirty-five minutes.

Sunday, August 25, 1929

"SERVICE IN THE GROVE"

IT WAS a perfect Sunday for Mrs. Caldwell's picnic.

Reverend Kreuz was still on his holidays, which meant no church service for our congregation. The outing at Caldwells' Grove in the afternoon was something to look forward to although I wasn't forgetting that its *raison d'être* was religious. Indeed Mrs. Caldwell's "Service in the Grove" was still church, albeit with a slight difference. There was to be a ball game, maybe two; and lunch in the open under the trees was always twice as enjoyable as elsewhere.

I spent most of that Sunday morning reading the "Young Co-operators' Page" and the "Torchies," then I sorted stamps and Elsa helped me take the paper off the backs of them. We hadn't done this for ages. I did things that particular Sunday that I hadn't done for a year. Church at home or elsewhere with Reverend Kreuz had so monopolized my time that I wasn't used to being at loose ends like this. After lunch we piled into the big car, the "good car," and picking up a couple of Kaschls we headed for Caldwells' farm.

Because of the crowd we had to park our car in the ditch and walk the last three hundred yards. There were vehicles from twenty and thirty miles away. Missenden's ball team, the Hustlers, and a gang of rooters were easy to pick out in their snazzy uniforms; the Clarendon ball team had named themselves the Clarendon Wild Cats to strike terror into their opponents' hearts and were also there with their supporters from across the valley.

Mom was lucky: she joined Mrs. Tischler, an ardent baseball fan, who had arrived early enough to have their car parked behind home plate where she could watch the games. I went with Dad and the "little kids" for a short walk around the grounds. Mr. Caldwell met us once, wearing his Sunday best, bareheaded and in his shirt sleeves. He was grinning like a cat full of chicken and he winked at my Dad when he passed him as if they were sharing an enormous joke.

Excitement was everywhere! Mrs. Caldwell's benches and tables were already set up in the grove where lunch would be served after the first game. Mothers were darting off here and there looking for their kids, or taking them out behind the bushes . . . The Caldwells' one outhouse was working overtime with the crowd on hand that day. Already by three o'clock one had to pick his way gingerly through the trees . . . No doubt Mrs. Caldwell had made a mental note of that . . . That was a shortcoming to be rectified by next year . . .

Young couples were walking hand in hand; "Chuck" Wilson from up near Missenden was riding around on his prancing horse, dressed in full cowboy regalia, lapping up the admiring glances of the youngsters from Minby, Clarendon and Missenden who had never before been this close to a real cowboy. Then I ran into Erik Haugen, so I left my Dad, and Erik and I went off by ourselves.

We passed Donald Grenz from Missenden who, as usual, was alone. He was the doctor's son, a kid I had always envied and wanted to talk to; he had probably gone along with his Dad dozens of times in that new snowmobile! And I'd heard too that they even had a beautiful big player piano, the best one you could get in the city; one of the Kaschl kids told me too, although I don't know how he found out, that Donald even had his very own "shetling" pony. Erik didn't like Donald at all; he said that he was a stuckup little bastard, "like most of the kids from Missenden" and that he just thought his "shit didn't stink," that he was "too good for anybody in Missenden, let alone in Minby.'' That could well be, I still wanted to talk to him; but what Erik had just said about him summed up what I thought of Erik himself, but was there any point in telling him that?

We met a couple of old granddaddies excitedly jabbering away in Russian or Ukrainian and we watched while one took his plug of tobacco out of his back pocket, and traded a chew from it for what was left of the other's cigar. We saw democrats and buggies tied up to the fences or to the trees, and as often as not a dog was lying down in the shade beneath waiting to go back home again. A couple of teenage boys from Missenden were driving around on spanking brand-new bicycles with red, white and blue crêpe paper woven in between the spokes on both wheels, thus adding a patriotic touch to the day. They were all C.C.M.'s, exactly the same model old Mr. Stephenson had promised me for helping him with his invention. Did Missenden have an inventor too, one whose Pot O'Gold was in closer reach than Lionel's?

There was the whole Heywood family, the sour-looking father, the patient mother, and six poker-faced kids all sitting silently in their big car, just as it had pulled up two minutes or two hours before — it was impossible to tell. There they would sit motionless, the scowling father, the patient mother and the six poker-faced kids until the *fun* was over when they would head back home. Their procedure today was the same as on a Saturday when they came in to Minby; the parents did the shopping for the week in remarkably short order while the kids sat silent and motionless in the car, not even talking among themselves. Then they went back home again. Mrs. Haugen remarked to my mother that they looked like ''well-brought-up kids.'' Angèle said they were just ''too ascared'' of the old man to open their mouths; and to believe Angèle, who could pick up the most fantastic bits of information — most often true — Mr. Heywood used to beat his wife regularly, invariably adding her incredulously dramatic, high-pitched "and just something awful!"

There were two or three big cars with American licenses, either visitors from the States, or the absentee landlords themselves who had come up earlier in the spring to do their seeding and were still around, or owners who had just come up to see how their crops and their tenants were doing. There was Dr. Grenz himself, Donald's Dad, from Missenden with his brand-new Graham Paige. He didn't keep a new car very long — wasn't he driving a big McLaughlin-Buick touring something like ours only newer a couple of weeks ago? How long would he be able to watch the game today before being called away again on an urgent case? There was . . .

But I didn't get a chance to see who all it was, Erik had turned around sharply, pulling me off in the exact opposite direction — he had just recognized his Dad with Emil Pedersen from Missenden. Why should Erik not want his Dad to see him? or why should he always appear afraid and avoid him? Would his Dad *really* care if he had seen him? And here I really liked Mr. Haugen, I thought he was a real good sport, no matter what Erik might think. If I had to choose between the two why I'd . . .

A sharp crack, followed by cheers, informed us that the ball game had just started, so we hurried over to the improvised diamond. Some ball enthusiasts insist that the players are only at their best on a sweltering hot day. This Sunday was a scorcher, and a good one for the ripening wheat. There was a constant run of noisy chatter around the bases and coming in from the field to the Missenden pitcher before and after every ball he threw. The first man up who had gotten safe to first, died there when the next three batters struck out; now it was Missenden's turn to bat.

The noise from the crowd was deafening. After a few minutes warm-up, Missenden's first batter was up. Walt Crippen, who was umping today, called the first "s-t-r-i-k-e o-n-e." The Missenden man at bat acted surprised and took his revenge on the very next ball the pitcher sent sizzling over the plate and knocked it for the only home run of the game. Thereafter the remaining eight innings were tight, with two or three on base practically every inning when the third out was made. Reluctantly we saw the finish of that game: one nothing for Missenden. It was time for lunch!

Already a few of the buggies and democrats were heading for home although it was still early in the afternoon. In spite of the early departures there was still such a crowd that the Ladies Aid couldn't cope with serving the huge number left. They had never had so many before. Everything was sold out before half the queue had been fed. Mrs. Caldwell had probably made a mental note of that too for next year. Mom resigned herself to making supper when we got home after all. Well, I thought, rubbing my hands, we mightn't *have* to stay for the church service either . . .

But we did stay. At least for the beginning of it . . .

With lunch over, the men began knocking down the tables to be now used as benches in front of the spanking new platform. Mrs. Caldwell was "My, my-ing" smugly all over the place, wondering where she was going to put all "her" guests *next* year. The new platform looked imposingly grand — all that brand-new lumber, and with the big tent-like baldaquin set up over it! People were asking one another where Mrs. Caldwell got that kind of canvas from, for wouldn't it have been *her* idea?

Mr. Caldwell could have left off the tent part of

the platform, it wouldn't be raining today! Nor would the sun bother the parson when it came time to preach. A rope, no doubt to separate the improvised stage curtains, at the head of the stairs to the platform, was moving ever so slightly in the breeze.

So *this* was Mr. Caldwell's surprise! Pa had undoubtedly been over earlier in the afternoon to inspect his handiwork, for without his long iron braces that platform wouldn't have held together.

No one had seen the evening's guest speaker yet, but Mrs. Caldwell assured everyone he would be on the train in Missenden at six o'clock and that Mr. Caldwell was on his way that very minute to meet him, and — great news for the kiddies! — they were hanging up Japanese lanterns complete with real candles in the trees, and these would all be lit up later on in the evening *right after* the service was over! Certainly a delicate thought on the part of *good* Mrs. Caldwell, someone was saying, "Such a hard-working, self-sacrificing soul!" added another. Maybe she was making sure that the crowd would stay — for if enough kids wanted to enjoy the treat of the lanterns, wouldn't the parents have to stay for the service too?

And so the second ball game took place. Missenden's team had had a bit of lunch, they had all rested up and had no trouble adding a second victory to their laurels for the day. Clarendon's ferocious Wild Cats, in spite of the warning of their uniforms, turned out to be a bunch of tame little kittens.

The sun was setting . . .

Mr. Caldwell had arrived sometime before with the Reverend Meredith Bryce-Windsor, B.D., and everyone was now getting ready for the service to start. The last of the crowd was dribbling over from the makeshift diamond to the improvised benches. There wouldn't be nearly enough of them, the men would have to stand.

Mr. Caldwell, however, made one slight miscalculation in his plans for the evening, he hadn't *quite* the audience participation he had counted on for *his* surprise. He, a good Scot, should have known that the "best laid schemes o' mice an' men gang aft a-gley."

Mrs. Caldwell, clucking busybodily as she nosed around here and there, making her last inspection, was trying this, checking that for the dozenth and last time. She spoiled her husband's plans by pulling the rope and parting the curtains of the platform marquee about a quarter of an hour before the service was to start, before all the crowd had made its way there, thus depriving the majority of the people of the spectacle that her self-sacrificing husband had so carefully prepared. He had really given his all, *literally* offering himself to provide the special event for that year.

As Mrs. Caldwell, irritated, was fussing with the rope, the rope that *he* was supposed to have checked, it seemed to stick. Her attention was focused on the little pulley through which it had to pass and where it seemed to have caught. She was vexed, annoyed . . .

She gave another jerk, an angry impatient one this time and the curtains fairly flew apart. She heard the women scream. Following their horror-stricken eyes up to the platform itself, she could see her husband's limp and lifeless body as it slowly swung back and forth beneath the protecting canvas.

An overturned chair was beneath it.

THE HIDEAWAY

I ALWAYS loved to walk, and whenever I was free I would hit out on foot: north, east, south or west, it didn't matter. I often went with Erik Haugen's Dad when he was out of a job, or with Erik himself if we were on speaking terms. I generally stuck to the country roads because I knew the farmers. Who knew — I might get a ride with a team and wagon and be allowed to drive for a mile or two; or I might get a ride with one of the grain trucks which were becoming more and more common. I'd had dozens of rides with Old Jack Smythe. He'd stop and ask me to hop in before I even waved him down. Once I even got a ride the last three miles into Minby with Vic Armstrong on his bike. He was on his way in for his music lesson from Mrs. Tischler. It was hard on the seat, but it added to the variety of my walks, which was a large reason why I liked walking. One never knew . . .

That particular Saturday I had made up my mind to go out south for a mile, hit due east for two miles and cross the valley; then I'd head north for two miles, west two miles and the mile south, crossing the valley once more and so back into Minby. Eight miles on the square. I had the whole afternoon ahead of me. I was prepared to walk the whole distance but was sure I'd get a ride part of the way.

The first mile south went according to schedule. The road was dry and dusty, the day cool for September from an overcast sky. I turned east and covered just over a mile and a quarter, crossing the tracks, and was about to dip down into the valley. Did I really want to take so long a walk? The sight of the steep road winding up the hill on the far side three-quarters of a mile away was intimidating. I changed my mind and decided I didn't want to go so far after all and after a few moments' hesitation I turned back. I'd do my eight miles another time.

I could have retraced my steps completely, going west and then north the mile back into town. Instead I got off the road and began following the edge of the valley hill in a vaguely northwest direction. The terrain was dry and dull, the rare cactus patch faintly visible and here and there an animal skull. I was never sure whether they were cows' skulls or buffalo skulls, though Dad assured me time and again they were practically *all* buffalo skulls, and had been there for years. Away down below me I could see Bennett's Aberdeen Anguses grazing quietly. The big old bull off to one side reminded me that this part of the valley had been dark with buffaloes not more than sixty-seventy years before — so Dad was always telling us.

I was startled once by a late gopher and wondered what it lived on since there wasn't a wheat field within half a mile. Ever since I had been out poisoning with my Dad, I was sure gophers ate nothing but grain. On and on I went, slowly, leisurely, somewhat aimlessly, since instead of six more miles to go, I would have less than two to cover before being back in Minby. With a rattle and roar the freight train clattered by me on my left as it headed south. I kept on walking, gradually approaching the railway tracks. I could choose between cutting directly over to them, or following the edge of the valley around. It would be a littler longer until I hit the road coming in across the valley from the north if I took the latter course, but that was far more interesting than following the tracks.

I was about to go down into the ravine when only a few steps down the slope I could distinguish a door lying against the hill, sheltered and partly concealed by saskatoon and chokecherry bushes. The "dumps" or nuisance ground as they were also called, were a mile further on; had this door fallen off or been dumped here by mistake?

But was it just a door? As I looked at it, I saw there was a frame around it, and that it led somewhere. Just a few weeks earlier, when the bushes were heavy with leaves, the door — it was painted a dark green — would not have been noticed. It was hardly a job of camouflage because no one came this way — only my chance decision to make a short cut had brought me so close to it. The longer I looked at it, the plainer it became. I recalled the story in school about the Pied Piper of Hamelin and how he had caused a door to open into the side of a hill and how he had taken the children away with him. I had had that story once from Mrs. Milford too, long years before I ever heard it in school. It would have had to be a door something like this, only about twice as wide.

Of course I was too smart to run straight over, in case someone was watching me. I took a seat in the grass where I could see it out of the corner of my eye. Maybe, like Robin Hood's men, they had sentinels watching.

Knowing I was on the threshold of some great discovery, I was alternately excited and fearful. Should I sneak back to Minby and get Erik or Louis to come back with me? Not Erik — not this time, I was a bit peeved at him. Half the time when he knew something I didn't know, he'd tease me with his I-know-something-you-don't-know refrain until I offered him some stamps he had been wanting just to get him to tell me. No — I wouldn't ask him — another time maybe. Louis Kovacz? Hardly . . . Saturday was Kovacz's busiest day in the store — Louis would be up to his knees in eggs getting them repacked for the afternoon train.

The longer I sat there and pondered, the itchier I got and the more the mystery deepened. What could it be? I decided to take a short cut directly to the tracks which would take me within a few yards of this enigmatic door. I slowed down when only a few feet from it. For a moment I expected one of Grimm's fairy tale witches to come out after me and put me behind this door and fatten me up like the one did in "Hansel and Gretel". . .

The door was fastened from the outside, not with a lock, but with a hasp and staple, with a substantial twig holding it shut. I took a step closer, cleared my throat a few times like my Dad did, loud enough to warn anyone inside to come out, but no one came. How *could* one come out with the lock on the outside? That reassured me.

I was soon down under the bushes and examining the door at first hand. What an ingenious arrangement! It was plain to see, once I was beside it, that someone had been there recently, the heavy twig holding it shut was green and the bared space on it still moist and a lighter green where the bark had been rubbed away. Someone had jammed it in that very day. Enough people had trod the earth under those overhanging bushes to free it of grass and weeds. I knocked, feeling it was a stupid thing to do; I knocked a couple of times, looking around to see if I was observed. I cautiously withdrew the twig and slowly opened the door.

How often hadn't I dreamed of having a secret place all of my own, exactly like this one, or an island like Robinson Crusoe's where I could run off all by myself! If I could have furnished my secret hideout, I would have done it exactly like this one. It was the neatest, comfiest, coziest room I could imagine, quite adequate, although a full-grown adult would have had to crouch slightly to get in. Here I was in a room literally dug into the side of the hill, about six feet high, seven feet wide at most and about ten feet long. The walls and ceiling looked to be shored up with old grain doors, the floor was hard-packed earth. A squat, potbellied stove with cut-up neatly stacked wood beside it for fuel, proved that whoever used this place, used it in winter too, though there was no pipe visible from the stove to the ceiling. Had it been taken down for the summer? Maybe they came only at night *when it didn't matter* . . . One long bench was fastened solidly against the wall and a rude table and two captain's chairs completed the furnishings.

There was a newspaper on the table dated August 24. Today was September 21. Somebody had been there the month before. My heart did a little flip when I realized that August 24 had also been a Saturday, the Saturday exactly four weeks previously. Maybe "they" only came on Saturdays. "They" had just been here, the twig in the door told me that — it was fresh. Would "they" perchance be coming back again *today?* Were "they" perhaps on their way now? In much less time than it had taken to open the door, I was out, had it closed and the little twig shoved back in and literally "hit the tracks" for Minby.

I slowed down about halfway home and tried to think a bit more rationally about this discovery. Who, in all Minby, could *possibly* belong to a secret society, for didn't it *have* to be a secret society? If not, then why hadn't I known about this place long ago? How many belonged to it? Judging by the size of the room, the size of the table, the number of chairs and the size of the bench, hardly more than four or five — half a dozen at the very most. Was it some murderer's hiding place? But there hadn't been a murder in Minby for years — in Missenden, Yes! but in Minby, *No.* Were they dressed in white robes like the Ku Klux Klan we had been hearing about at home? like this guy Hawkins — so Dad said — who was up from the States trying to stir up trouble in our part of the province?

Did these guys, on the other hand, have something to do with an underground movement? Not just because their little house was underground . . . I had read about undergrounds in some of my stories for getting colored slaves away, but the Jubilee Entertainers at the hall before Christmas had said that that was all over, that slavery didn't exist any more even though something as bad had been left behind.

Could we have some sort of "Injun Joe" in Minby, one I knew nothing about? This *really* puzzled me, for didn't it *have* to be someone I was maybe seeing every day? Who? Reg Hopkins? Mom and Angèle said he was "always up to some of his tricks . . ." Jack Fender? No — not Jack Fender. Would Old Jack Smythe have anything to do with a hideout like this? I'd have to start watching everybody a little more closely, even my friends . . . But all that seemed so impossibly far-fetched. I was absolutely confounded and concluded that the smartest thing was to hold my tongue. I would make the most careful inquiries possible. Not a word to anyone, not for a while anyway.

NIGHT PROMENADE

IT WAS Erik's idea that we thumb a ride on a gravel truck. They had been hauling for the past few days, graveling the main dirt road between Minby and Missenden to make the first all-weather road in the province. It wouldn't have occurred to me to ask one of the drivers for the ride. Trust Erik Haugen to come up with an idea like that to get up and back for nothing.

With the exception of about a mile and a half, the road the trucks were now graveling would form part of the *new* highway. Two new curves, one a mile south of town, the other just across the tracks, were put in, rounding out the two existing ninety-degree turns, and Pat Crippen swore that he could take them both with his New Model A Ford at *thirty-five miles an hour!*

It was well after supper when Erik got this big idea; we stood out on the road twenty minutes before one of the strange drivers picked us up. He was ready to drop us off as we came into Missenden half an hour later, thinking, no doubt, that we were Missenden kids bumming a ride *back* home. We said we wanted to go right out to the gravel pit with him and see how he loaded up — that was the main reason why we had come along. *Then* we would drive back with him to Minby.

"Back to Minby? Are you kiddin'? Hell, I ain't drivin' back to no Minby tonight!"

What a feeling in the stomach to hear this! How would we get back home? The driver was indeed going out to the pit to put on a load; that way he would have an early start the following morning. But there would be no more trucks hauling that evening because the checkers were done work an hour before. We would do better to get right back out on the road and try hitching a ride, *any* ride to Minby, before it got any darker.

That put an altogether different light on the situation! An hour earlier we were biting our fingernails in impatience because we couldn't get a ride to Missenden. Now we were cursing ourselves for our stupidity in not making sure we could get back.

If I had only had brains enough to tell Mom where I was off to! How often had Dad and Mom told us kids this! I was prepared for a good bawling out when I got home, maybe worse. If we weren't picked up by some car, it would be hours before we could be back in Minby if we had to make the whole of the return trip on foot. Minby was nine miles away.

Erik, put on a brave face, but his lips were quivering. He was scared to death of what his father would do to him when he got home. Erik was two years older than I, but he was two inches shorter, an insult to his Dad who would have preferred a son tough and belligerent like himself. Thank heavens it was Erik's idea that we come and not mine, or he would be blaming our present predicament on me. I, on the contrary, felt on such good terms with his father, that I was sure I could go home with him and take the blame if necessary.

And so we set out.

The first mile back went rather quickly. Maybe it was just because we were fresh; maybe it was because of the small diversion that the signs along the road offered us. We could see and read, in reverse, the work of the enterprising Missenden sign painter, admiring it for the distance of four telephone poles: "and a comfortable room," "for fine foods," "the Missenden Hotel and Cafe" and "Stop at . . ." There was the distraction of still other signs, of the Whistle Post on the track, the Yard Limits sign, the Mile Post to tell us that we had covered a ninth of the distance. When a slow freight lumbered by heading towards Minby, I would have given anything to have been able to hop on. Erik started to cry.

"We'll never get home!"

"Keep looking ahead, don't keep looking back!" I said "As long as you keep looking at the bloody elevators in Missenden you'll never think we're getting any place!"

I could hear a roar coming up behind us, from a big cloud of dust. It was Mr. Mitchell, our teacher, in his brand new Oldsmobile. It was a big maroon two-door sedan. For the first few days we all thought it *was* his — the new 1930 model that sold for $1,165! — but word got out that he had somehow persuaded one of the dealers in the city that he could sell a few Oldsmobiles around Minby. All he needed was a demonstrator, a big one . . . The car he was driving was it. And so for the five or six weeks that he had now had the car — he never made a sale — he had been burning up the dirt roads around Minby and Missenden when he should have been preparing school work for his pupils. I recognized the car, I recognized him, it is even possible that he recognized Erik and me, but he just sailed past, windows open, his long hair flying, and the accelerator pressed to the bottom. Truly he must have been hitting sixty!

Erik was boohooing unashamedly. What a serenade to have to listen to! If he was going to get this awful licking, why not just save his tears until he got home — crying wouldn't get us there any faster.

It was getting darker. I could hear the characteristic putt-putt putt-putt of those new John Deere tractors, and sure enough one of them came up behind us. Slow as it went, it was still going a bit faster than we, and it eventually caught up with us. I asked if we could climb on and rest a while. But it seemed like it was only ten minutes when it turned off and we had to climb down and start walking once more.

Halfway . . .

Another freight train about a mile long, all empty boxcars, rolled slowly and noisily past.

Erik finally quit crying; he even went so far as to start a conversation to bolster his courage. That was better. Even though it was dark, he was quite sure that we'd make it back to Minby by ten and that was only an hour after he had to be home *anyways*. maybe he could fool his Dad into thinking he had just been sitting out in the yard.

We talked about school, we talked about what I would do when I "passed my Entrance" — Erik had passed his three years before — and Erik sprung another one of his ideas. He was the damndest kid for getting them! He was telling me how his Dad laughed while reading an account of how some Communists in China sent their kids to the Missionary Schools to get an education. It wasn't because the fathers wanted them to get Christian instruction, but it was an excellent way for them to learn English. On top of it all, the missionaries gave the kids dinner every day *to keep them coming!*

"That's what I'll do, by Christ!" said Erik. "I'll try to get into some Bible School, Bible College or Seminary, I don't give a damn what it is, if I have no other way to get an *eddication!"*

"But you can already speak English . . ."

"Yeah, but to learn something else," he answered.

"But what else *could* you learn in one of those places?"

Another car. It was going the wrong way.

"Maybe they'll feel sorry for us and drive us back to Minby," said Erik hopefully.

I hoped the driver had heard him, or read his mind.

We could hear coyotes howling in the distance.

We hurried along . . .

The faint light of a coal oil lamp in a window indicated

Scott McEachern's place. That meant that we had only about a mile and a half to go. Twenty-five minutes? We were making much better time after all, or the time was just passing quicker than we thought. I rejoiced that we might be home by nine thirty but my remark had just the opposite effect on Erik who started to cry. The closer we got to town, the worse he howled. Did his father really and truly beat him up like that, I wondered? Tired and a bit footsore, we crossed the tracks and then headed up dimly lit Main Street.

I offered once more to go along home with Erik, and he accepted. As it turned out, however, I didn't have to. Who should come staggering out of the Pool Room and Barber Shop but Erik's Dad and Emil Pedersen from Missenden, the two of them bleary-eyed . . . So intoxicated had I never seen Mr. Haugen before, he recognized neither me nor his son beside me. I don't think he even saw him. Erik, crimson with shame to see his father in this inebriated condition, would have preferred finding him sober, even if it had meant the terrible beating he had been talking about.

FOWL SUPPER

WE HAD the Fowl Supper that night. That night too I told Erik Haugen about the hideout I had discovered, for how could I keep the secret to myself much longer? Of course he let on that there was nothing to it. That night, too, everyone in town learned some rather astounding news . . .

The Fowl Supper, for once, wasn't the big financial success it usually was. The food was delicious as always — after all the Minby women were the best cooks in the country — at least that's what Reverend Robert Teakles, the guest speaker, said, although he had said the same thing about the Missenden ladies a few nights before. The program wasn't bad either. I played for Kerstin Göranson, who worked at Müllers' Hotel and who was roundly applauded for her numbers. So was Barney Grant when it came his turn to sing. Of course he included "Felix" with his other selections

Reverend Teakles acknowledged that the Ladies Aid hadn't had the success they merited, and he blamed the relatively poor crowd — poor in comparison to last year and the year before — on this new technical wonder having its preview in Missenden that night. They were showing the first 100 per cent talking, singing and dancing movie, *Broadway*. We had had posters all over Minby advertising it. There had been a half-page ad in *The Missenden Thunderbolt* with screaming letters two inches high: "Girls, Guns, Gangsters and Gigolos." Dad had been sorely tempted to forsake the Fowl Supper and take us to Missenden — he'd been reading everything he could lay his hands on about "talkies," but he didn't think a film about gangsters and gigolos anything to take us kids to.

"If they're any good," he said speculatively, taking his toothpick from his mouth, "and if *another* comes to Missenden, we'll be sure to go".

Another came. The talkies were here to stay.

Either the Fowl Supper in Minby or the talkie in Missenden should have been postponed, but the Ladies Aid wouldn't hear of moving their night. Hadn't they picked the date first? Had they not had their posters up for weeks? Hadn't they also put a special announcement in *The Missenden Thunderbolt?* Indeed, and they had even paid Mrs. Barry down at the Phone Office to put out a general ring when they began to hear rumors of all the people who were making plans to go to Missenden the same night to see *Broadway*. Gus Carlson, the operator of Missenden's Lyceum Theater said he would have willingly co-operated with the Ladies Aid; after all, wasn't it in his interests? But he had had no choice: he had to take the film when he could get it or show another silent, and who the deuce would want to see a silent film now? Weren't his customers driving twenty, thirty and forty miles over to Rottingdean to see a sound film?

Reverend Teakles had been to Scotland on a merited vacation, that is, *The Missenden Thunderbolt* reported it had been a much merited vacation . . . That had been his first trip back to his place of birth since coming to Canada, and his talk that evening was on his homeland. I had last seen him about four months before on the roof of my Dad's blacksmith shop building the brick chimney. He had been a bricklayer before getting his "Call" to go into the ministry. I wondered if Reverend Kreuz could do anything *useful* like that . . .

Reverend Teakles had brought back with him a bunch of lantern slides from his old home which he was showing; when he said he had one of Annie Laurie I perked up my ears. We used to sing "Annie Laurie" in school. There she was now on one of those slides, all dressed in white, a big white floppy hat to match, sitting out in the garden at her father's place. I couldn't see that she looked different from the women around Minby . . . The people smiled and I heard someone behind me say, "Why it's Mrs. Teakles!" and indeed it was his wife. Reverend Teakles could *always* be counted upon to inject *humor* into his talks . . .

I had told Erik Haugen just enough about my secret hideout to get him interested. Of course he wouldn't let on that he was curious. We had decided to thoroughly investigate this mystery at the end of the concert. Neither of us thought Reverend Teakles' lecture very interesting so we sneaked out of the hall when he said he was going to show us a picture of Bonnie Dundee. After his wife, hadn't we seen enough of his relatives?

Had I taken Erik directly to the hideout I would have saved ourselves our scratched legs and arms, and a lot of walking. As if the discovery of this retreat wasn't marvel enough, here I was trying to add still more mystery to it by taking him the longest, most indirect route to it. We each had a good flashlight, and off we went, but not down the track as we could have done; instead, I insisted that we take the north road out across the tracks and then head east down into the valley. It would be a long detour; then we'd double back along the river until we hit the ravine which would eventually take us up towards the track, allowing us to come in the back way. Erik said scornfully it would probably be a wild goose chase. When it suddenly got almost pitch dark and I didn't turn on my flashlight and refused to let him turn on his, then he got mad.

"What'd we take 'em along for *anyways?*"

"We can't turn 'em on here. Wait a while! When we're in the hideout underground we can turn 'em on all we like. If you do it here they can see you from half a mile away!"

And so we stumbled along up the hill, through rose bushes, gooseberry bushes, saskatoons and chokecherries. A few times we could hear and see dark shapes moving, but it was only Bennett's cows. It took three-quarters of an hour just to get from the river up to the ravine. When we were almost at the top of the hill a startled owl flew up silently and swiftly only yards from us scaring the two of us so badly that we had to stop for a few minutes.

"It's just up ahead now," I whispered encouragingly after a short pause. I was now sure of my bearings.

"Where? I can't see nothing!"

"Sh . . . I think I hear somebody!"

I thought I had heard somebody not too far from us, and for fully five minutes the both of us stood petrified, like statues, scarcely breathing. Should we go ahead or turn back? I decided to go ahead but it wasn't because I had suddenly become brave. The fact was that the prospect of retreating all the way down the hill into the pitch darkness appealed even less to me than going on.

It was getting later and darker with every passing minute. Looking uphill and into the sky was much better than casting a fearful backward glance into the murky depths below. So, making as little noise as possible, I inched my way forward until I was practically at the hideout door. I stopped and listened, no voices were audible. The only sound I could hear was the rumblings in my intestines, my breathing and the thumping of my heart. I was right beside the door, I could feel the bit of wood still shoved through the staple, exactly as I had left it a few days before, exactly as I imagined it would be.

"Come on," I whispered to Erik, and before he came up I had the door open and had clambered inside. I turned my flashlight on.

There, on the table — hadn't I seen it a hundred times before? — was the concretest clue as to the identity of the occupants of this hideout. I should have hid it to save face, but my brain didn't work that fast. Had Mr. Kaschl, the section man, ever forgotten his lunch kit before? Going or coming from work he always had it with him, it was as much a part of him as was his sober weather-beaten face and his pipe with the funny little cap over the bowl; but this day he had left his lunch kit behind. It was a big, rectangular, dark-blue-mottled box, a most distinctive lunch box, the only one of its kind in Minby — maybe he had brought it over from the Old Country with him. Since Erik had seen Mr. Kaschl as often as I, then he had seen this lunch box too, for the two were inseperable.

What I had stumbled on to, what I had known nothing about, what Erik also knew nothing about, was the section gang's little hillside dugout. Did every section gang in the province have as much fantasy as Minby's? The Minby gang had dug this little room out of the side of the slope and had been adding little improvements to it over the months. Was there any reason to broadcast its whereabouts to the public? It was a cool comfortable spot where they could eat their lunches out of the summer heat and perhaps have a hand of rummy before going back to work; more important, it provided a cozily sheltered haven, once the fire was built, where they could eat their lunches and warm up in the winter. Had I only taken a closer look that first day I would have seen that the neat stack of wood by the stove consisted of old sawed-up railway ties. Erik, always one to belittle, reacted in his traditional scornful, jeering manner when I confessed that my first conjectures had been all wrong.

"I knew all the time," he lied. "I just didn't want to let on."

That time I got damned good and mad and gave Erik a kick in the ass, the first time I had ever come to blows of any kind with him. After all, in spite of his age — he was two years my senior — he *was* smaller than I.

Of course we were disappointed at not finding at least one badly wanted robber sound asleep whose hands we could have tied, or whom I could have bravely held at bay while Erik ran off to phone the police . . . As we slowly walked home thinking and talking about this little place and what it might have been, our thoughts were on gangsters, murderers, blood and thunder. We were therefore ripe for the news that had broken that same evening in Minby during the concert. Erik and I had left a few minutes too soon.

Mrs. Caldwell had of course stayed on at "her" farm, even after her husband had made such a spectacle of himself by stringing himself up that Sunday evening. She had counted on ending her days there nevertheless with her annual Sunday Service in the Grove . . . She was having a soft water cistern put in her basement when Jack Fender who was helping do the job quite by accident discovered a most ingenious gadget that Mr. Caldwell had contrived. It was to have blown up the house and to have set it on fire when the furnace was first lit in the fall.

So Lionel Stephenson wasn't the only inventor that the Minby district boasted; Mr. Caldwell was another of the same breed! Only Mrs. Caldwell's better angel (?) had spared her and her girl from certain death, for apparently Mr. Caldwell had been quite prepared to sacrifice their daughter too, the child he hoped was "all hers," when he set out to even his score that day.

THE LAROCQUES

THE LaRocque kids started school several weeks after everyone else that year. They weren't Minby-born like us Viggos. Where, exactly, they had come from I don't know, other than "somewhere on the other side of the lake." There were half a dozen of them. The two oldest ones, Jeanne and Stan, I knew quite well — they were not only in my room but in my grade. This fact would have been surprising to anyone not knowing their background, since Stan was more than two years my senior, and his sister three or four years older than he. They were neither stupid nor retarded, none of the six LaRocques was, they had just grown up in a district where they had scarcely had the chance to go to school. Their Dad couldn't stay put very long in one spot either, which didn't help matters any. Now they were making up for lost time.

Jeanne, who looked older than she was, seemed to be even older than Miss Chatwin. She looked every bit as old as Mr. Mitchell, the principal, and was very self-conscious about her age. She was determined nevertheless to get a bit more schooling; besides, what else would there have been for her to do out on the farm?

It's doubtful that Mr. LaRocque found a thing to do the whole time he was in Minby — our little village just didn't offer much employment opportunity. He squatted with his family on a little piece of land, the most derelict piece of land, probably the poorest, most miserable piece of land in the whole municipality. It was only part of a quarter section to begin with, mutilated by the hills that led down into the valley, and by the railway line which traversed it diagonally; what was left was unfertile. Mr. Montague, whose quarter it adjoined, said the whole section of land should never have been touched with the plow. This was the so-called "Old Pringle Place." The Pringles had unwittingly baptized this quarter by homesteading there twenty-five years earlier, though they stayed no more than a year. They were only the first of many families whose paths led them for a time to Minby and who found temporary refuge there.

Jeanne distinguished herself one of the first Fridays she was at school. The only high point in our long and monotonous school week was Friday afternoon when, at three o'clock, we cleaned off our desks, put away our books and had the weekly Literary Society. We had an elected program committee, of course. Sometimes we recited, but mostly we just gave readings, we sang, we even had a school newspaper, *The Clarion*. And when Mr. Mitchell came back in the fall he announced that after these Friday Literary Societies he would give a critic's report, and indeed for the first two weeks he did give a three minute résumé; but when he realized that his second was identical to his first he gave it up. At three thirty we were freed by the bell until the following Monday morning when another monotonous school week began.

One Friday after the LaRocque kids had been there a few weeks, it was either Jeanne's turn to come up in front of the class, or she had just volunteered. We really sat up and took notice because she chose not the little four-line, four-stanza doggerel we were used to, but a real masterpiece of elocution cut down to our size. This she recited with such polish, conviction and emotion that she carried the whole room with her from the beginning of her selection to the end. She was as much a perfectionist in her field as Kerstin from the hotel in hers when she sang. Of course she was often called on after that. Like Kerstin, she delighted in doing what she could and in sharing what she had; she wasn't "showing off," she just performed.

Jeanne always wore either a purple dress or a black one as she stood in front of the class. One arm she held down by her side, about six inches away from her body, glancing down from time to time as if looking at a paper in her hand for a helping word. But she never had to use notes — this was just her mannerism, the stance she adopted while we settled down to a comfortable position in our desks, the same way a pianist sometimes sits for a few seconds to compose himself before playing. We knew it would be good, and we prepared ourselves too.

Jeanne was lonesome. She would have welcomed company, but she was much older than the Grade Eight girls and had little in common with them. They were already moving in a tight little world of their own of boys, surreptitious dates, dances, jokes, the latest smart repartee ("I'm from Missouri, yuh gotta show me!") and the latest jazz hits. Jeanne had an inferiority complex in their presence, since she was only in Grade Six, and for this reason she spent practically all of her time by herself at recess, morning and afternoon, five days a week, week after week . . . She probably wouldn't have found what Babs Cantelon and Daph Lautrec had to talk about so very interesting anyway. Moreover these two "flappers" spent their recesses with the teachers in the library.

Now Jeanne was not beautiful; she was squat and heavy-set, with thick gray-black, dead-looking hair and a blotchy complexion. She looked as if she could wash and wash herself and still never get clean. If you were unkind, you could say she was downright homely. These facts we all forgot, when she began reciting. She was so convincing in her actions when she gave direct quotations that I turned my head more than once to get a look at the person she was addressing. Afterwards she would lend me the texts, and I read them eagerly, but never with the same delight as when I had heard her. The element of surprise was gone and what I imagined in histrionics from the cold text couldn't compare with her lively rendition the Friday before. I asked her once where she had learnt all these items, confessing I had never heard the likes before.

"Oh," and she just laughed off my compliment, "you should hear mother. Mother taught me all the things I know!"

From that day on I wondered what her mother was like if the daughter's performance, by her own admission, was such a faded, colorless copy alongside. Jeanne had nothing but praise for her mother as a teacher. When had I ever heard anyone talk so enthusiastically about a parent? But where would *I* ever get the chance to hear *her*? Did she belong to the Homemakers? Did she belong to one of the Ladies Aids? Did she belong to the Southern Star, to the Legion's Women's Auxiliary or any of the lesser organizations in Minby that might ask her to recite at one of their concerts? The answer was "no" to all these questions. I was one of the exceedingly rare people outside of the LaRocque family to just *see* the mother the whole time they were in the Minby district. She never once came to town to shop, she never once attended a function in the Minby Community Hall, not even the Christmas concert in which her own children participated.

To see and hear Mrs. LaRocque! That, in just a few weeks, became an obsession with me. I pestered Jeanne long enough for her to say, "Well, why don't you come out to our place some time?"

That was an invitation Jeanne was never to repeat, an invitation she probably never meant to extend in the first place; and if she meant it, did she think I would follow it up? It was an invitation I stored away, nourished and savored for weeks, keeping it in reserve, awaiting a favorable opportunity.

I assumed, since the rare times the Viggos visited or had company was a Sunday, then Sunday was really the only day I should go to the LaRocques. But since I was generally occupied every Sunday myself, now that I was playing organ again, it seemed I would never have the chance. But eventually one Sunday did come when Reverend Kreuz's plans took him away alone and after our own morning service in Minby I was free, free, free . . . Oh what a wonderful afternoon it would be, the delights of which I would prolong leisurely, enjoying them in little licks like an all-day sucker! I would have an unhurried Sunday dinner at home for a change, after which I would go out to the LaRocques. I had thought of leaving at one o'clock; but Mom convinced me I should wait until at least two.

"Just because we eat at twelve o'clock is no reason to think everyone else does," she said.

Somehow I waited the extra hour . . . Then I was off, their shack, the smallest, the most squalid and decrepit in the district, shining off in the distance like a fairy-tale palace.

I set out on a slow run, but before I was halfway there my heart was in my throat. I could see the house all right, but in the quiet air theirs was the only chimney with no smoke coming from it. Weren't they at home? I plodded along halfheartedly nevertheless. I stopped at their gate. Yes! There was a faint whisp of smoke coming from the smokestack after all! Only a hundred yards to go; I was all atremble, quaking in my boots with doubtful anticipation, behaving more like a lover on his first date than a young kid hoping to meet an older schoolmate's mother.

I could now see their dog at the side of the house
and its bark informed me that someone was at home
and should have informed them that a stranger was passing along the road. I turned in. The dog continued to
bark; I got to the outside door and knocked. So few
people must have dropped in that they probably mistook
my rap for some other noise. I knocked again and again,
frantic now, and *finally* heard another door inside open
and hesitant steps approaching through the shed to let
me in. It was Jeanne. She was absolutely dumfounded
when she opened the outside door. I didn't even say
"hello" . . .

"I came to hear your mother!" I blurted out.

"Well!" She waited a full thirty seconds, adding hesitantly, "Well, come in."

I followed her through the cold shed into the house.
The curtain to the bedroom was still moving slowly as
if someone had just beat a hasty retreat before we came
in. The room, a combined kitchen-dining-room-parlor,
was almost in darkness. I could see the glow of a cigaret
in the corner and the vague outline of a man lying on
a cot. He reeked of tobacco. It was the father. He grunted
as I came in, the only sound I was to hear from him
that afternoon. A brother and sister to Jeanne were quietly
sitting by the small stove, and through the broken bits
of mica in the stove door the meager fire could be seen
glowing within. It wasn't much, but I would have sworn
I preferred one like that which you could see to our
big warm furnace back home . . . They had evidently
been reading until it got too dark. They said a bashful
"hello" and that was the extent of their conversation.

What strange household had I gotten into, I wondered, thinking I hadn't done the right thing by coming.
Presently I heard the scratch of a match in the bedroom,
and from the pale wavering light behind the curtain I
knew a coal oil lamp had been lit. I felt extremely foolish

for having come, wondering what I should say or do next. Jeanne, although right in her own home, wasn't a bit "at home." Indeed she was as tongue-tied as I, as much out of her element as I out of mine. We needed the familiar surroundings of the school, the *Medalta* drinking fountain in the corner, the blackboards, the ink-stained desks with the initials carved in the tops, and, above all, the smell of chalk and dust-bane to loosen our tongues . . .

The curtains parted, and there, holding the small lamp in front of her, was Mrs. LaRocque. Could she have made a more dramatic entry into that room if she had been an actress playing a part? If Florence Nightingale herself had been asked to portray "The Lady with the Lamp" could she have struck a more striking pose than Mrs. LaRocque's? She was more like Jeanne's older sister than her mother, so much like Jeanne's older sister that I could have confused the two of them since I immediately recognized the purple dress, the *other* one . . . Jeanne had on the black. Were they the only two presentable dresses they had between them?

"You must be Wally Viggo!" she began breathlessly. "Jeanne has told me so much about you!"

She was laughing and shaking hands with me all at the same time. Her black eyes sparkled in the dim light just as Jeanne's did when she recited at school. She had so much animation in her voice and in her gestures that the whole poorly furnished room came to life; everywhere I turned now there were dancing shadows cast by the wavering flame of the coal oil lamp. The children loosened up a bit more too now that their mother had come into the room, and indeed the room seemed warmer from her presence; the hard chair I was sitting in suddenly felt as comfortable as our big rocker back home, and this fascinating woman in purple who bubbled over with merriment enchanted me.

One person in the room took no notice of what was going on — the husband: stretched out, motionless, only a hand moved now and again to relight his cigaret or roll another one, and only the glowing tip when he took a puff indicated that he was alive and breathing.

We talked about Books, and Mrs. LaRocque took her lamp over to her little library. Books, evidently, made life livable for her in this wretched, miserable shack. There were four or five plain shelves about four feet wide with their well-read contents now in view, Canadian authors mostly, some of which I had read before. About a third of one shelf was devoted to Ralph Connor. I thought I had read everything he had written but here was one that was unfamiliar to me.

"Can I read this one?" I asked.

"Why of course!" said Mrs. LaRocque generously. "But you must take good care of it, it's Arthur's."

Arthur? That wouldn't be Mr. LaRocque, would it? I knew those of her boys at school, and none of them went by that name.

"You can just give it back to Jeanne when you've finished it."

And a few minutes later . . .

"Of course you know that Ralph Connor was really a minister down in Winnipeg. Ralph Connor was only his pen name, his real name was Reverend Gordon."

"What," I thought to myself incredulously, "Ralph Connor *wasn't* Ralph Connor? Ralph Connor *hadn't* written his books? A minister had written these books?" And I wondered if Reverend Kreuz could ever write a book, he whom I had never once seen reading one.

"My grandfather helped build the church he preached in!" Mrs. LaRocque was adding enthusiastically, maybe a trifle boastfully.

I couldn't believe my ears! I wanted to reach out and touch Mrs. LaRocque's hand, this woman who had practically walked and talked with God, for Ralph Connor, *even if he was a minister* as she had just said, was at that time my favorite author. I had borrowed *The Foreigner* and *The Doctor* from Dad's friends the Lundbergs not too long before, both of which I had read twice; and how many times hadn't I read and reread that tear-jerking passage in *The Sky Pilot in No Man's Land?* And as I clutched *To Him That Hath* in my arms, this one book of Ralph Connor's that I still hadn't read, I was almost impatient to get home and into it.

Mrs. LaRocque showed me an autographed copy of *Flint and Feather* and she said that once, long, long before, she had heard Pauline Johnson read some of her poetry. This book was Arthur's too . . .

But wasn't Mrs. LaRocque going to recite? After all, wasn't that my main reason for coming out?

I brought up Jeanne's elocution at school once or twice, mentioning how much we had all enjoyed her contributions to our Friday programs. I thought, having introduced the subject in this manner, that Mrs. LaRocque would recite, or that Jeanne would perhaps take the hint and ask her mother to. Jeanne didn't take the hint, and reciting seemed the farthest thing from Mrs. LaRocque's mind that day. Finally I made the suggestion.

"Oh, I never recite for less than five hundred!" she said and she laughed as if that was a tremendous joke.

"Five hundred dollars?" I gasped incredulously.

"No," she laughed in merriment, as did her kids — this was evidently one of her old jokes, "for five hundred people!"

Nothing I could say or do, nor could the collected efforts of her children who also wanted to hear her — no, *nothing* would make her recite even the smallest poem for us that afternoon.

All good things must end. I had supper with them, which I ate exactly as they did theirs, though I wondered what my parents would have thought had they seen me: a thick slice of homemade bread thickly spread with butter; this I placed on my big dinner plate, poured my cup of hot sweetened tea over it, just as they did theirs, and ate it with my spoon, imitating them once more. It was delicious . . .

"We have our big meal at noon," explained Mrs. LaRocque with a friendly, confidential smile, but she wasn't fooling me. I had seen enough in the house and from the kids' lunches at school to know that if I had come at noon they would have their big meal at night.

Mr. LaRocque, who still hadn't moved from his couch, was noisily ingesting his tea and bread in his corner, reclining like Lucullus on his divan after being served.

After a last glance over their library, I also borrowed the collected works of Pauline Johnson, which Mrs. LaRocque told me I must be very careful of, and with my arms full of books I set off for home.

"Good gosh, kid, don't you know when it's time for supper?" was Mom's combined greeting and friendly bawling-out as I came through the door.

It was away past eight o'clock. I had been gone over six hours! It seemed like two or three.

Some weeks later when I returned Mrs. LaRocque's books to Jeanne, my curiosity got the better of me. I had noted on the first pages little inscriptions. In one, "To Arthur LaRocque, given to him on his birthday by his mother," and the date. In another, "To Arthur from his mother for being such a good boy," again with the date. Every time I read those little dedications to Arthur I wondered which of the LaRocque boys was the book-worm and proud owner. I finally concluded it couldn't be any since none of their first *or second* names fit; I had checked the school register to see. When I asked Jeanne who Arthur was she was very embarrassed but finally told me it was her mother's first born, a boy who had died.

"Just before you came to Minby?" I asked, remembering some of the dates. "What from?"

"No," said Jeanne, more embarrassed than ever, "he was the first one, he was older than I, I never saw him, he only lived a few days . . ."

Just like "our" Waldemar Erik, I thought, the oldest one in our family, the one whose first name I now bore. A *little* bit like Waldemar Erik . . . If Mom still saw her first baby boy as he was at four months, smiling down to her from the enlargement of the snapshot taken only a short while before he died, Mrs. LaRocque's little fellow on the other hand was just as much alive as her living progeny, celebrating birthday for birthday with them. He was probably *more* alive, for had I seen a single dedication to one of her living children?

I went out to the LaRocque's place again. It was some time later during the holidays and I asked Erik Haugen if he wanted to make the little trip with me. I regretted extending the invitation to him immediately. I had always wanted to like Erik and often felt sorry for him. He was about the loneliest kid in Minby. Actually he should have been Kalle's friend, because of his age, but Kalle wouldn't have a thing to do with him. Kalle insisted that Erik was a little sneak. He *was* a bit of a sneak, I agreed there, but a lot of the things he did just *looked* sneaky. And he was such a skinny little runt — wringing wet he didn't weigh seventy-five pounds. But there were times when his "see-I-know-it-all" attitude got my goat. I would no more than start telling him something when he'd interrupt, "Yuh, I know," even when he didn't know what I was talking about. For weeks at a time we wouldn't speak but he'd always outwait me — I was the one who "made up" even when the fault of our tiff had been his.

I had mentioned the LaRocque home to Erik, both the LaRocque parents, and especially Mrs. LaRocque. When he scoffed at my remark that Jeanne's mother looked more like her sister than her mother, I felt like giving him a kick on the right cheek of his little ass; and when he just as scathingly doubted that Mr. LaRocque could really spend the *whole* afternoon on the couch without moving or speaking, I wanted to give him the mate to the first on the left . . . Wasn't he calling me a liar, the little . . .

This day, about a week after the school concert, we set out. Erik had been just as impressed by Jeanne's delivery of "The Night Before Christmas" as I, and he looked forward to hearing her recite something else.

In the summer we could have taken a short cut through the field; because of the snow now we followed the road. There was no smoke coming from the chimney.

"See, I *told* you so!" Erik jeered, "There's nobody home!"

Erik hadn't told me anything . . .

I insisted we go on, I hadn't seen much smoke either the first time I went out.

When we were a hundred yards from the house I admitted that it didn't look very promising. There was no sound of a dog barking, there were no tracks of any kind in the yard in the fresh snow from that morning. I had a sinking feeling in my stomach — I knew, this time, that there was no use knocking, but I went up to the door and rapped anyway.

No one came . . .

Nor did anyone come the next day or the next. The LaRocques weren't just away for the afternoon, for the day, or for a holiday; they had picked up and moved on once more, just as noiselessly and unobtrusively as they had arrived only a few months before.

"You knew all the time they weren't there, I betcha!"

I didn't pay any attention to this irritating little runt; all I could think of was poor Mrs. LaRocque, her wretched little shelves of books, her kids, of Jeanne, of Arthur . . . But above all of Mrs. LaRocque herself.

IN DAYS OF YORE . . .

IN SPITE of my New Year's resolution to make the most of my time in school, my books couldn't keep me interested. How frustrating and stultifying to come to the school and just s-i-t from nine till twelve, and again from one till three thirty with just a short recess break!

If only we had had something to do! I tried not to waste my time, but my mind was forever wandering back to my younger happier days (a whole five or six years previously . . .), the majority of which I had spent at this very same desk, in this very same room.

I thought about old Mr. Dorritt, my first teacher. He had been back to Minby once or twice his first year of retirement, but he died the following year. Dad always insisted that if Mr. Dorritt had kept on teaching he would have lived to be a hundred.

I thought most often however, about Miss Fraser whom I had had the next two years and who had taught us so many beautiful songs. I could turn around in my desk and see the big empty space at the back of the room now where we had played our musical games. She had married Barney Grant, who also loved music.

I loved Miss Fraser as did the majority of the pupils, but she had had a mortal enemy in Henry Smythe. When Miss Fraser, at a loss to reach him otherwise, finally asked him why he didn't like her, he couldn't (or wouldn't) tell! Two incidents concerning Henry stood out very clearly, epic in proportion I used to think, in both of which I figured though not too actively, and I'd find myself reliving them when I should have been doing my work.

Henry was sure that Miss Fraser didn't like him; she bawled him out a few times, but then she reprimanded anyone who dawdled or fooled around. He was positive she had it in for him. They say that babies and dogs can tell instinctively when they're not liked. . . Maybe Miss Fraser *didn't* like him, her protestations to the contrary. One day at noon, when Miss Fraser returned to school, Henry was waiting for her. In his hands, armed much like a soldier with his rifle and bayonet, he held the three-tined pitchfork from the school barn. The very second that Miss Fraser got inside the school grounds he rushed out of his hiding place, and holding the fork like a Tartar's lance, he met her on the double. With a shriek Miss Fraser was off in the other direction, running much faster than her tight skirts and high heels ordinarily permitted. She fell once, had time for one glance at the raging fury coming up behind her, regained her feet and was off again like a startled doe.

Most women really don't run ladylike; for purely physical reasons they throw their legs out like a cow . . . Miss Fraser, that day, ran neither like a lady nor like a cow; she pulled up her skirts and ran like the batter who thinks he's hit a homer and is trying to make home. She was terrified; she didn't know which way to turn, and finally didn't turn anywhere but just kept running in a circle. She had long since lost her lead, and Henry was just close enough behind to give her a jab in the posterior when in reaching distance with his fork; that was enough to set her off again as if she had been given a charge of electricity.

I then performed the only courageous act of my life. I'll call it courageous although I had had time beforehand to weigh all the possible consequences. Henry, I knew, had nothing against me, and if I got into this to help Miss Fraser, the worst he could do to me was blacken an eye, bloody my nose, or give me a crack with the pitchfork. When they came around the next time, I moved in close enough to throw myself under Henry's fork and into his feet, thus upsetting him. The chase was over.

Miss Fraser earned our collective admiration by pulling herself together, dusting herself off and strapping young Smythe. It should be added for the record that she had the co-operation of Henry's older brother who ordered him to take what he had coming or he'd tell their "old man." The "old man" was Old Jack Smythe of course. Old Jack might have looked and acted like a venerable and benevolent patriarch in Minby but he was a holy terror at home. Since Henry knew what to expect from the old tyrant if his brothers or sisters did tattle, he submissively accepted the strap.

Even after the punishment Henry fancied he still hadn't heard the last of it. Miss Fraser promised him a brand new slate, saying he should forget his grudge, insisting he had had no reason to bear her one in the first place. So one day when she had forgotten to lock her desk, Henry took the strap out of the drawer and hid it behind the clock over the blackboard.

The clock, without being anywhere near the size of a grandfather clock. was one of those with a visible pendulum, a big face with Roman numerals, and an octagonal wood frame around it; but between this octagonal frame and the wall was a small square flat wood box, out of all proportion to the size of the clock, which housed the "works" of the timepiece. Henry had draped the strap over the "works" box, between the octagonal frame and the wall to which it was attached. It was safely concealed. Had it occurred to anyone standing directly beneath the clock to look up to try to see it, he couldn't have. All that was visible were the two ends, one hanging down each side; but since the strap was gray-black in color, the area between the frame of the clock and wall always in semi-obscurity, it was effectively camouflaged and doubly secure. But not secure enough for Henry, although it would have taken an earthquake to jar the strap from its hiding place.

Miss Fraser missed her strap, but adopting a "wait-and-see" tactic, she said nothing; she had taught long enough to know that sooner or later she would hear what had happened to it. One day Henry found his secret too much to carry alone and he confided in me. Now even if I had had nothing to do with putting the strap behind the clock, I felt just as guilty as he. He couldn't keep his eyes off the clock. When Miss Fraser caught him gazing at it one morning only ten minutes past nine and told him to get to work, he made up his mind. . . At noon when Miss Fraser and all the town kids were away home for lunch, watching his chance when the classroom was empty of country kids too, he took the strap down and put it not in his pocket (he didn't have one big enough!) but inside the knee breeches he habitually wore, right next to the skin; there it must have burned until three thirty when school let out.

Waiting for me at the door, he grabbed me by the hand and soberly commanded, "Come with me, Wally."

I suspected it would have something to do with the strap, but I couldn't imagine what. We went to the boys' outside toilet and only half-closed the door so we would have plenty of light. There he undid his belt and unbuttoned his breeches. I, obviously, *had* to see this. He hauled out the strap from alongside his leg, held it dangling over the toilet hole much as if he were holding a two-foot garter snake by the tail . . .

"Say good-bye to it, Wally," he commanded once more.

And laughing the same devilish sort of laugh I had often heard from his Dad, Old Jack, he let it go.

Now I was let in on a worse secret than ever. Knowing the strap was behind the clock had been bad enough.

My first desire now was to unbutton my own trousers and get up over the hole . . . What an urge to defecate! Could I have felt guiltier if I had taken the strap in my hands and dropped it?

"And if you say one word to anybody, I'll knock the livin' Jesus out of you!" he added with the same note of menace I had once heard in Old Jack's voice too.

Overnight Henry's show of bravado reached heroic proportions in his own mind because before school next morning he opened up to two of his friends about it; they, of course, were not to tell a soul . . . By nine o'clock there were enough little snickering groups whispering and giggling in the schoolyard to confirm that everyone, boys and girls alike, now knew the fate of the strap. If Miss Fraser eventually learned what happened to it, she said nothing. Henry behaved thereafter — that was all that mattered.

Everywhere I looked about me were reminders of things past. My mind for the last year and a half had either been dwelling on the "good old days" when I had been happy in school or, on the contrary, I would waste my time contemplating the future when I would have this entire unhappy two-year period behind me. Certainly Saturday School, when every other pupil in Minby except those of our congregation was free to do as he pleased, counted for a big part in my violent distaste.

Mr. Mitchell never gave an assignment; Reverend Kreuz, on the other hand, never missed giving his "homework," week after week. Catechism was as inevitable and as impossible to avoid as measles, whooping cough or any other youthful scourge. In addition, Reverend Kreuz came regularly to our home, invited or uninvited, a constant reminder to me and to my parents — to my mother in particular — that these lessons had to be learned for this Saturday, the one to come, and the one after that. For two years, if Mom wasn't asking me if I had practiced my hymns for Sunday, she was asking if I had learned my catechism for Saturday.

Added to the torture of Saturday School e-v-e-r-y weekend, were the still wearier Sundays, all day long, when I had to accompany Reverend Kreuz in his weekly trips to his other congregations. It was a never-ending task, like the barrel in the fable that had to be filled. No matter how many Sundays I managed to plug, there would be another to fill the following week.

"UNCLE" MARTIN

AFTER only a few years in Minby "Uncle" Martin, Dad's Old Country friend, spoke an impeccable English, made friends easily, and considered himself one of the village's sporty business men. He had a gift for picking up languages and could exchange more than just casual greetings with his customers in German, Ukrainian and Polish. If Minby had ever had a Board of Trade, or a Chamber of Commerce, "Uncle" Martin would have been its president for sure. In and out of his office he presented a dashing figure. That was particularly so when he dressed to play tennis with the "bank bunch." That, too, was before Minby's banks closed, the one last year, the other the year before: white shirt, white trousers, white socks and white tennis shoes, what dashing figures they all presented!

Even as a kid I used to wonder how these people — particularly "Uncle" Martin — could be free to indulge in this sport at four o'clock in the afternoon when my Dad, Mr. Stewart, Mr. Kovacz — in short when all the other business men in Minby were tied to their businesses until 6 p.m. — later still Saturday nights. I used to see them several times a week in the summer since the tennis court was across the road from our house, in the leveled-off space of the open-air rink which would be flooded for skating when cold weather came. The prestige the bank employees enjoyed from their jobs must have made up for their inadequate salaries — only "Uncle" Martin used to reward me with a nickel for retrieving the balls knocked over the fence out of bounds.

I used to visit "Uncle" Martin regularly in his office before Reverend Kreuz appeared on the scene, at least once a week, perhaps even oftener. He imparted to me my deep and abiding love for mathematics. At the *very* first, I think, "Uncle" Martin somewhat resented what I learned, for there were times I know when he, "hoist with his own petard," was slightly jealous of the rapidity with which I picked up some of his best tricks. Once he realized that he could bask in the reflected glory of what I, his star pupil, might perform, he set about teaching me all his short cuts. It didn't take that long, by the way . . . When I demonstrated my new-found prowess to his farmer customers — for I was as incorrigible an extrovert as "Uncle" Martin himself — he showed me off (and himself . . .) like his trained seal, taking credit for what he, as he invariably added, had "taught the kid."

What all did this mathematical wizardry involve? Frankly, not a great deal — nothing more than adding fractions ("in his head" Martin would always explain), multiplying by twenty-five (also "in his head" . . . which was very simple since Martin's short cut just involved adding a couple of ciphers and dividing by four), multiplying by eleven (also a trick anyone can duplicate once he's been told how). Where the kids in school were expected to know their multiplication tables to 12 times 12, "Uncle" Martin persevered with me, drilling me by rote, until I could go up to 16 times 16. Why not beyond that point? Perhaps because that was his own limit.

With his natural flair for mathematics, "Uncle" Martin, as one might expect, could also play cards and he passed his repertoire of games and tricks on to me. Above all he introduced me to cribbage, or just "crib," at which he generally beat the pants off me. When I didn't win a game, he'd give me one so as not to discourage me. Until one day . . . That particular afternoon when the combinations of "fifteen-two's," the double runs — in short when an appreciation of the odds in discarding, cutting and pegging became crystal clear in my subconscious, I was suddenly able to beat "Uncle" Martin at his own game, not just once, but three games straight. That was a turning point. It was the beginning of a marathon that continued for over a month and went on every time I came into his office when we played as many as five games — he would either tie me, or the game would finish with me one game up. After a grand total of forty-seven games in this manner when "Uncle" Martin *finally* got one ahead, he threw the cards down, and red in the face from the emotion and strain — he had been waiting for this moment for several weeks, he said:

"There now! Do you *still* think you can play crib?"

"Sure," I said, eagerly grabbing the cards to tie him again. With luck and a "skunk" — a skunk counted double — I could perhaps get one ahead.

But "Uncle" Martin had had enough. It was the last game of crib I played with him that day. It was the last game of crib I *ever* played with him . . .

There were other aspects of "Uncle" Martin's office that intrigued me. "Uncle" Martin sold coal and wood and, depending on the season, would let me weigh the empty wagons, sleighs or trucks when they came in, and again when they were loaded, and I calculated how many tons of coal were on. I had practice in what "Uncle" Martin jokingly referred to as "monkey-plying" when I would figure out for him what the load was worth. This bit of knowledge permitted me to help him on more than one occasion, for now and again he'd leave me in the office while he sneaked off for half an hour or more for a quick one with Reg Hopkins or Rudy Guschlbaur.

All my pastimes in "Uncle" Martin's office weren't quite as innocent as those card tricks, "crib," and the mathematics problems, although they could still be considered educational. Without having read or heard of Rabelais or Boccaccio, "Uncle" Martin was a disciple of what those writers "taught." He chain-smoked and had puffed and inhaled his Millbank cigarets so energetically and so long that he had accumulated two complete sets of the pictures called "Perils of Early Golf" which he had received in exchange for his tobacco cards. One set he left as he received it. The other he doctored up with his colored pencils. These pictures were of Scots in kilts, golf balls on thistles for tees, the players precariously teeing off with poisonous snakes or a brontosaurus within easy snapping distance . . . If there might have been some doubt about the sex of these wild creatures, or the golfers themselves when "Uncle" Martin received the pictures — they were about 10″ by 14″ — there never was on the second, his "personalized" set, *after* he had finished doctoring them up. It must be admitted that his artistic talents were superb in this domain.

A hilariously similar *chef d'oeuvre* but in considerably more detail involved a big "Old Chum" tobacco calendar. Two pink-cheeked, white-haired "Old Chums," long-stemmed pipes in hand, were obviously discussing the merits of their favorite tobacco. Their upper torsos were visible, appropriately garbed in a Dickensian manner to match their white wigs and jolly smiles. Beneath them was the large outsize calendar itself which was fully as wide as the picture above. On the white space behind the "December" sheet, however, "Uncle" Martin had completed the drawing of the two old chums but he hadn't put their trousers on — he hadn't even put any underwear on them . . . If certain of the Minby folk spoke in hushed tones about Reg Hopkins and his "hidden virtues," they couldn't have held a candle to those of "Uncle" Martin's two unassumingly smiling old Englishmen.

"Uncle" Martin also smoked a pipe. He didn't *really* smoke a pipe — that was only the pretext he used to keep buying the hip-pocket-size flat red tins of Prince Albert pipe tobacco. He liked to demonstrate how he could scratch out certain letters on the back of the can with his penknife to leave the following text: "Pa covered Ma to produce me and Pat." Since he generally gave the empty tin to a farmer as a souvenir (and, no doubt, to remind the recipient what a clever chap he, Martin Eriksson, was) he had to recreate the text on a new can each time he *extemporaneously* showed a customer his versatility in this field.

Now and again I would surprise "Uncle" Martin in a deep study. This, I concluded after a time, was when he was concentrating on what his *next* bit of deviltry could be.

If "Uncle" Martin told *risqué* stories in my presence, there were nevertheless certain things he didn't divulge. When you knew "Uncle" Martin as I felt only I knew him, you realized the restraint exercised on his part. For example . . . I was all of nine or ten, — that is, only a year or two earlier — before I caught on to what he really meant when, with a grin, he spoke to one of his farmer customers about his "work table." Always, when he made that reference, it was accompanied by a wink or a smirk, maybe the two, then a loud guffaw, as he indicated with his foot a narrow mattress which he kept under the counter and which could be pulled out into the middle of the office floor. Had it had the gift of speech, that pad could have given a detailed report of what kept "Uncle" Martin busy those evenings when he worked overtime . . .

"Uncle" Martin liked to drink and although he didn't know I knew it, he kept a two-quart sealer of homebrew cleverly cached between the big scales and his counter. He was certainly one of Kass Komos's best customers before Kass got caught. How many liked their homebrew the way "Uncle" Martin drank his? He would throw a handful of Christmas candy into the sealer, shake it around a few times, and that bit of sweetening was sufficient (at least that was my interpretation when I was able to sneak a swig of it) to cut the raw brew to make it palatable. "Uncle" Martin liked beer, too, which was a bit of a bother after he'd had a few bottles. The problem of running back and forth to the outside toilet he settled efficiently by utilizing an empty coffee tin which he kept in the adjoining room and which he would empty every second or third time out the side window.

"Uncle" Martin had the patience of Job, and it was this more than anything which enabled him to indulge what might be termed his "quirk." "Uncle" Martin's was simply this: he was a "leg" man, but not in the modern, "newspaper" sense of the expression. . .

By standing at the extreme end of his counter and looking slightly northeast past the end of the Old Hotel, "Uncle" Martin could see the two-seater *shiddis* that had originally belonged to the Old Hotel (now closed) which was used by farmers' wives and town women alike as a rest-room. If Max Harrison was particularly fascinated by the sight of a buxom woman's breasts, "Uncle" Martin, on the other hand, was enthralled by the sight of a woman's leg, thus proving that *all* tastes are permitted in nature. "Uncle" Martin was unusually gratified if he could catch a glimpse of a little of what was above the knee.

"Uncle" Martin had an excellent Eastman Kodak with a remote control and this, with only a few seconds' notice, he could solidly mount on his counter, the lens pointed directly at the Old Hotel toilet. He would wait . . . and wait . . . and wait for some unsuspecting female to head for the privy, and snap her, first — if he was quick enough — as she was stepping up to get into the emergency edifice; then, like a spider with a fly in its web, Martin would keep his eyes on the toilet door, waiting for the first move of the handle to tell that his victim was ready to come out again. He had pictures of half the women in the district of Minby as they cautiously stepped down, some looking to the right, others to the left. But one, his pride and joy, he prized above all and it was, to quote "Uncle" Martin, "a daisy." It was Mrs. Tischler, my old music teacher, as she held the door frame with one hand for support, her face screwed up in a frown, peering off vaguely to the right to see if anyone was watching her as she stretched her leg down to reach the step below. Ordinarily this would have constituted a worth-while picture in itself, on a par with the best "Uncle" Martin had snapped until then. This one was different: Mrs. Tischler was unaware that she had inadvertently tucked part of her dress into her panties (and what panties!) as she made herself presentable again. Since Mrs. Tischler was one of the largest women in the district, this somewhat compromising picture, to quote "Uncle" Martin once more, "did nothing for her." "Uncle" Martin claimed that he had had a standing offer of $5 for that snap from "Gentleman" Max, which seems rather strange considering Max's very special tastes.

When word got back to Mrs. Tischler — as it did to *all* the women thus immortalized, for wasn't that half of "Uncle" Martin's fun? — she said testily it was "a bit too much" and she vowed to get even.

But how could Mrs. Tischler, out on her farm seven days a week except for Saturday afternoons when she gave her music lessons — yes, how could she ever hope to settle an account with the likes of "Uncle" Martin? She didn't broadcast her feud with him any more than

Old Jack Smythe his with Mrs. Red Blaine — yet everyone in the district knew about the two of them.

Like Old Jack, Mrs. Tischler was patiently biding her time.

I'LL SEE YOU AT THE MASQUERADE

I HAD never been to a masquerade. They were rare in our town, generally held Leap Year if they were held at all. The tall tales I had heard about the one held in the Old Hotel, before the Minby Community Hall was built, left me seething with impatience when I saw the posters advertising the one on Friday. The Minby Agricultural Society was putting it on, and since most of the farmers supported this organization, a good crowd was assured.

A full day before the dance, smoke could be seen coming out of the hall chimney. That was unusual! I had to investigate . . .

"*Wanna* earn a dime, Wally? Or are you going up to practice your hymns?" said Jack Fender when I stuck my head in the door. He had once surprised me playing jazz on Bethel Tabernacle organ and never let me forget it.

In ten minutes I was handing him pins as he fastened yards and yards of streamers together. I cut more crêpe paper for even more streamers until my hands were sore, I moved chairs this way and that, and I moved them back again. I pushed benches around until I was blue in the face; I was up and down the platform forty times as I carried pliers to this person, a screwdriver to someone else; I was here, I was there, I was everywhere — in short I was Angèle's *mouche de coche*. One by one the men left for their evening meal. When I left with the last one I was sure that without my help they would never have managed . . .

Seeing those decorations go up was but a preview of the masquerade to come and far from dulling my appetite only whetted it the more. This was just background! What would it be like with the hall lit up and the dancers there in their fancy disguises? That was all I could think of next morning in school. Even the Friday afternoon Literary Society, the only high point in our monotonous school week, couldn't interest me this day. I squirmed in my desk with impatience — all I had on my one-track mind was the big dance this evening. Hadn't I single-handedly got the hall ready for it?

"So they're not letting kids in tonight!" said my sister Elsa, keeping a straight face at the supper table to test my reaction.

"Have you practiced your hymns for Sunday?" asked my mother, throwing a bucket of ice water over me and my enthusiasm. In my preoccupation with the coming dance I had completely forgotten. Well, that would give me something to help fill in part of the time . . .

"Have you learned your catechism for tomorrow?" Mom asked when I was home from Bethel Tabernacle again, letting in another blast of arctic air to cool me off once more: Unpleasant tasks, like misfortunes, never came singly . . .

I had learned my catechism a few days before, but it didn't hurt to review; but my mind was miles away from things spiritual. All I could think about was the masquerade; I knew that when I got big enough to dance I'd go to a masquerade too, and I'd go as the devil, with a diabolical face, horns, forked tail and all, and I'd be all dressed in red . . . Which shows how Sunday School trains one for the Social Graces after all . . .

At seven thirty, an hour and a half before the dance was to start, I was in my Sunday best and champing ' at the bit. I could see the lights in the hall, and I knew that only the janitor was there, but I was impatient to go anyway.

"There's absolutely no use going over until nine o'clock, kid, and even that's too early, the crowd won't be there before ten," chided Mom.

I didn't want to see the crowd at ten, I wanted to see them come two by two, savoring each costume singly. And so I went and waited. I was more than a bit perturbed when they finally began dribbling in. The majority were only wearing their usual dress for a dance! Didn't they *have* to come in disguise? And could a costume be called a disguise when they weren't even wearing masks?

Of the first to come were two of Minby's young old maids. Neither could have been more than thirty-five, but the odds were very much against them. The one was almost square and looked like the back end of Mr. Stewart's big new Hudson. She had the same impact too when she collided in a dance. She could have been called Miss Five-by-Five, was truly immense and getting bigger and bigger as the months went by. She had really been christened Bertha and ever since the end of the war was referred to by everyone as "Big Bertha." Now it looked as if she was doing her best to live up to this name.

Bertha's cousin and inseparable companion, Daisy, was as tall and skinny as Bertha was squat and fat, and she had been like a fish out of water since the Standard Bank closed the fall before, now absorbed by the Canadian Bank of Commerce. Keeping the entries in her books straight had taken all of her time; her life, then, with her dozen ledgers and never-ending entries, had had as much meaning for her as Mrs. Kaschl's with her dozen kids and eternal housework. Bertha had kept books too, but for the Dominion Bank across the street from Daisy's. It had closed the year before.

The two ex-bank employees sat hopefully side by side, gold-painted paper crowns on their heads, gold-trimmed masks over their eyes, each holding a gold-painted tapered stick about two feet long with a tinsel-edged gold star on the end of it. Were they fairy god-mothers like the one we had seen when the Live Wires enacted "Cinderella"? If only they could have reached over and touched one another with their magic wands and, by some miracle, have had their collective weight more evenly distributed between them! But the gods weren't gracious, and the swains of Minby heartless. The two girls were seldom asked up to dance, not even by their own brothers, and their brothers weren't prizes either. Not even "Woddy" Lautrec would invite them out on the floor, he who could be counted on to do a certain number of what he called his "duty" dances in the course of the evening, blissfully unaware that many of the women responding to his "Shall we struggle?" regarded their dance with him as a duty dance too. They, too, had certain obligations with regard to his mother who belonged to their church circle, the Homemakers, or some other such club.

Daisy and Bertha got up valiantly in every circle two-step, every time there was a promenade, one of the two doing yeoman's service pushing the other around when there was an Allemande left but even then the odds were that the two would be once more left on the floor when the signal "Everybody dance!" was given. They would soon be joined by Kerstin Göransson. Kerstin, seven or eight years older than Bertha and Daisy, was the third of this manless trio.

But who was this fat person disguised as a colored gentleman with a mask over his eyes and smoking a corn-cob pipe? He would have been an appropriate partner, size-wise, for Big Bertha except that they wouldn't have been able to reach one another. Big Bertha could just stand still, of course, while he danced around her. He smoked, exchanged words with no one. Not even "Uncle" Martin could get any response from him, and he was just *dying* to see who it was.

As the boxes arrived they were displayed at the far end of the hall in all their ingenuity. One enterprising lady had spent days on hers. It was huge, in the shape of a battleship, complete with gray funnels . . . And there were gasps of amazement when what appeared to be an enormous pie came in to be raffled off! It was made on an oversize plate of some kind, with thick whipped cream piled high over it. A Boston cream pie? A cake? Not really a box, argued the purists.

Then came the two teachers, Mr. Mitchell and Miss Johnstone, the new Junior room teacher. They had sent away to the city and had rented Spanish costumes for the big night. They looked the part, he daringly Ramon Novarroish with his long hair completely out of sight under his black Spanish hat, she like "loop-the-loop" Velez, a real Señorita. As long as Hildebrandts' old-time orchestra supplied the music, however, they would get no closer to a lively tango rhythm than Chris's corny sax playing "Silver Bell."

The whole "East bunch" arrived together. They always arrived together, danced together, ate together and went back home together. Tonight they had come as "hard-timers."

More boxes piled up. Two white square ones, almost identical, could be seen side by side. They were both even tied with the same green ribbon; one would swear they had been made by the same person. Or twins. Or had Bertha and Daisy brought them? That seemed hardly likely, for hadn't those two old maids arrived long before?

Then came the prize winners of the evening, an old Indian couple. Their disguises were perfect, sewn from gunnysacking and so expertly fitted and tailored with headdresses and masks so well attached that it was useless to peek to see who they were. Any skin visible below the hair line as well as that of their hands and wrists was appropriately colored. They didn't miss a dance, they danced together, they did circles, they never seemed to tire, they danced "old-time" and they danced "modern" — that is, what with a considerable stretch of imagination could be called "modern" coming from the Hildebrandts. Of course they would have to be one of the younger couples . . .

"Good Heavens!" gasped Mrs. Anhelliger. "Is that *really* Verna Law coming in the door, big as a house?"

"You'd think her mother'd keep her home, or send her East," was Mrs. Kripps' acid reply.

"Yeh," replied another, "if'n it was your Meda, or my 'Laine, Mrs. Law wouldn't never let us hear the last of it!"

And as the women speculated on the paternity of the unborn child Verna was so pregnant with, she found herself a seat in plain view of everyone. She had come to dance.

Then there was that "Damned bunch from Missenden."

"No," the President of the Minby Agricultural Society said, "trust *them* buggers not to come dressed," forgetful that more than half the Minbyites, including himself, weren't in disguise either.

The group from Missenden however, men and women alike, had condescended to put a brilliant patch of rouge on their cheekbones. Perhaps as a means of identification for later on . . . For if they were a very tight, homogeneous little group of eight when the evening began, dancing almost exclusively among themselves like "the bunch from out East," they, as the evening advanced, got tighter still.

And so they had circle two-steps, one only fifteen or twenty minutes after the dance started, to "mix 'em up." The President of the Agricultural Society wasn't doing his ulcers any good when he persisted in watching and calling attention to "the damned Missenden bunch" who wouldn't conform, who refused to be mixed up, who would dance off into the corners by themselves rather than join the circles. The two hopeful spinsters frantically got to their feet each time one of these "mix-'em-up" dances came along, the one of them *manfully* shoving the other around.

I couldn't keep my eyes off Woddy Lautrec between the dances. "It must be awful to be a runt like that," I said to myself more than once, although it didn't seem to bother him. Maybe being a runt makes Erik Haugen behave the way he does half the time too, I thought. During the dances when Woddy was up you couldn't see him because everybody including his partner towered over him a good foot, sometimes more. All you could see in effect was his partner who appeared, from a distance, to be dancing a solo, pulled first this way then that as if by some unseen hand.

There must be two or three like Woddy in every district who not only think they can dance, but who are first on the floor. As soon as the music starts for the next number, they, still back at the stag line, start doing a foolish little jig all by themselves like a loose-jointed jumping jack; and they keep it up as they start heading for their partner . . . Jim Grear used to do it too, until he overheard Old Carwardine say, "And he's even lighter in the head than he is in his feet."

Woddy wasn't in disguise for the masquerade, he didn't have to be; but all he would have needed to carry off the prize was a little red cap on his head, a cup in his hand, and a make-believe organ-grinder beside him. He was such a misproportioned and undersized half-pint

from the lower limbs down, that if he bent over, ever
so slightly, he could have touched the floor with the palms
of his hands. They hung loosely as he did his little dance,
he strutting around like a bantam cock before a harem
of hens. When one saw that stupidly euphoric smile cross
his face, it was plain to see that he was "Alkali" Willie's
cousin all right. His blond curly hair tonight, instead of
being plastered down and back on his skull, was freshly
shampooed, standing almost straight up with a heavy
shock of it piled up over his supraorbital ridge, almost
giving the illusion he had a forehead.

Immediately after one dance, it had been announced
that the one following would be a Ladies' choice. Angèle,
who had had that next dance taken with Red Blaine,
automatically got up to claim it, thereby incurring the
wrath of his jealously possessive wife. Mrs. Red, or
"Violence" Blaine as she was just as often called, asserting her rights as spouse no doubt, separated Angèle and
Red before they had been up on the floor more than
a few seconds. That Red Blaine was *her* man, and that
this was *her* "Ladies' choice" with him, Angèle or no
Angèle, was evident as husband and wife moved off,
she leading . . .

But what was the fat little colored man with the
pipe getting up for? And whom was *he* going to dance
with? This was Ladies' choice! In a minute we saw *him*
ask the Indian Chief for the dance. Two men dancing
together? Impossible! Was he a woman? And if so, who?

The view from the stage was the best, but the music
was grim. There were four violins, the drums and piano.
The four violinists were brothers, and the pianist was
the wife of Chris, the prodigy who doubled on C-melody
sax. The C-melody sax, of course, was for when they
played "modern" . . . Angèle said that the nicest thing
about the Hildebrandt music was the long pauses between
dances. That Mrs. Hildebrandt dared play in public, I

thought, was incredible and scandalous. Maybe even she was glad the other five played loud enough to drown her out. For the old-time dances she chorded, starting off with the chord in the appropriate key and finishing each four-bar sequence with the same chord, over and over again, regardless of what her music-bereft husband and her three brothers-in-law were playing. When they played "modern," which was about every fifth or sixth dance, she succeeded somehow in following along with the melody with one finger of the right hand, but the left hand just flopped around aimlessly, not even in time, and not too loud, on the lower keys.

It was amusing to watch for a few minutes, but painful to listen to. I therefore moved around to where I could have the beat of the big drum between myself and the pianist. The drummer seemed to be just putting in time as he slogged along, measure after measure. One might say he was the best musician of the group since he, at least, was always in key.

One of the violinists, the saddest-looking sack of the lot, had a longer, soberer face than Reverend Alvar even, and had, in addition, big bags under bovine eyes. He showed his versatility or individuality by playing for the entire evening with his fiddle halfway down his chest instead of under his chin like his brothers. And so he sawed away, hour after hour, as if he was resining his bow instead of making music.

The worse the Hildebrandts played, the more in demand they were. They were the only ones who could get steady dance jobs, since only they could play "old-time." The whole Hildebrandt family had come to our district in 'five but had homesteaded rather closer to Missenden than to Minby. Mr. and Mrs. Hildebrandt *senior* had supplied the music the first years until their boys took over, so actually the blame for what their sons committed could be fairly and squarely put on them — it ran in the family.

The Hall Board, the Minby Agricultural Society, and any other boards were comprised of the older men of the district all of whom had grown up with the Hildebrandt "boys," and the only music they therefore knew was the racket the Hildebrandts produced. To ask the solid citizens of Minby to listen to good music after the Hildebrandts, and to like it, was like asking the classical music public raised on Bach, Beethoven and Brahms to hear Schönberg's music for the first time and to enjoy it too. Improbable as it might sound to an outsider, the Minby Agricultural Society didn't set the date for the monster masquerade and dance until they were *sure* the Hildebrandts would be free to play that evening!

Immediately below the stage the two Schlachter girls were groaning to one another. Their Dad, his spectacles shining in the distance when he faced the Coleman lamp, had just come in the back of the hall to send his daughters home. He was taller than average anyway, and was now standing on tiptoe, his head making a slow turn around the hall as he looked for his girls. Indeed he somewhat resembled a parent bird peeking around the top of the nest.

"Shit, Myrt, there's old eagle-eye already," said the one sister to the other. "It must be eleven o'clock and the goddamned dance hasn't even got going!"

"No use squawking, Peg," replied the other. "Let's get down there before the old bastard comes down to get us here in front of everybody else. Maybe Ma'll sneak us out again . . ."

A fight broke out in the corner below the stage between Don Smythe and Steve Kowalschuk over Nancy Butler. For months now both had been courting that young lady. It wasn't clear who had brought her to the dance tonight, but it was clear to everyone in Minby why the two boys were interested in her, and why they were now battling unashamedly on the dance floor. Like a bitch in heat, while two dogs fight over her, she stood by unconcernedly, waiting to see which of the two would enjoy her favors later that evening. Clearly, it could only be the victor but Nancy was absolutely impartial, playing no favorite, pulling neither for the one nor for the other. Old Jack Smythe, Don's Dad, came over long enough to size up the situation, appraising with the eye of the part-time cattle buyer he also was the young woman his son was doing battle for, and to tell him for all in the hall to hear: "You needn't bother coming home after the dance if you can't beat the shit out of that square-headed bohunk!"

Before we knew it, it was the last dance; the boxes were being readied for the auction. They didn't have the customary Supper Waltz since each man was to eat with the woman whose dainty hands had prepared the lunch box he would be buying.

Hedley Cantelon, Chairman of the Minby School Board, was redfaced and in a rage. Fit to be tied, he was trying to figure out who was making a fool out of him because someone *was* making a fool out of him. He would no sooner get over one sneezing bout than his inquisitive nose would start sniffing around to see where it had come from, and to ascertain if there wasn't another little batch of powder coming his way. It wasn't lying — another little cloud wasn't long in arriving and he would start sneezing all over again. He bet it was "that damned Missenden bunch," adding they could "damned well stay at home" since Minby didn't need their "damned money."

Cantelon's own son, Buster, who sat behind me in school, and who was always up to the same type of trick there, and Cantelon's nephew, the same age as Buster, also in my room, were standing only ten to twelve feet away, backs to Mr. Cantelon now, like Peck's Bad Boys, busting their sides laughing as they prepared the next little charge.

And as the committee huddled off in the corner to figure out who had the best costumes, I could hear for at least the third time Mrs. Lionel Stephenson, wearing her big, floppy, oversize Leghorn hat, recounting once more the big incident in her life. Lionel Stephenson, her husband, Minby's inventor, lived in a world of his own, the centerpiece of which was his perpetual-motion-plus-power contraption upon which he had been working these many years.

Mrs. Stephenson was generally off in a world of her own too, even at the masquerade which should have been an escape from reality or from a second reality: she moved in a make-believe environment peopled with aristocrats, kings and queens, princesses, dukes and marchionesses, and she was relating for the hundredth time how, out in Victoria at this big reception in Government House to which she had been invited, the guest of honor was slow in appearing . . .

". . . and as I was coming down the steps, from the dressing room, my ermine over my shoulder, someone said 'Well that must be the duchess now!' "

I had heard Mrs. Stephenson say exactly the same words with exactly the same note of incredulity in her voice, and with exactly the same stupid look of childish pride on her face, many times before. She was so often in her dream world that it had practically become the only reality she knew. She had long ago given up cooking and the only things she ate or fed her transparent husband were aristocratic little bite-size sandwiches, macaroons and tea. She was obviously neither interested in the dancers nor in who would be selected as prize winners by the judges since she was paying absolutely no attention to what was going on around her. What, really, had brought her out for the evening?

One of the couples that had been outside to cool off filed back into the hall again. As they passed below me, I heard Mrs. Kripps tittering to Mrs. Anhelliger: "At least he could have brushed the snow off her back before they came back in . . ."

First prize, of course, went to the Indian couple. It was Mrs. Lautrec, Woddy Lautrec's mother, and Mr. Leslie, two of Minby's old-time residents. Gosh, Woddy was about twenty, his mother must have been about forty or more, and the way she had been dancing all night! Mrs. Lautrec and Mr. Leslie had abandoned their respective spouses for the evening, both of whom were in the know, of course, " to pull a fast one" on the rest of Minby.

Next prize went to the fat colored man who turned out to be a woman. Only her own husband had been in on the secret, a secret she had been able to maintain until the moment she took off her disguise. Since her husband never went to dances anyway, he had stayed at home that night too, both feeling that his presence at the hall would have given her secret away.

"Besides I didn't want him along anyway," she said with a lecherous wink.

It was Mrs. Tischler, the music teacher! She was well over sixty, fifteen or more years older than my mother.

"Why, she hasn't danced for twenty years!" exclaimed Mrs. Kripps.

The only dance she had had, she had danced with the Indian Chief, Mr. Leslie, late "forties," who had enjoyed an enormous reputation as a conqueror before he was married, and even now after celebrating his silver anniversary was still coasting on those laurels . . . Mrs. Tischler knew, if almost no one else did, who he was,

and was now enjoying her little joke. She said, for the
sole benefit of Mrs. Leslie, the "Chief's" wife, she had
"always been dying to get into his arms." Mrs. Leslie,
in spite of her sacrifice in surrendering him to Mrs. Lautrec for the evening, was known to be even more jealous
and possessive than Mrs. Red Blaine.

"Uncle" Martin was blushing as he tried to hide
his confusion. Hoping to pierce the fat colored man's
mask, he had invited *him* outside "for a leak and a drink"
only a half hour before the masks were removed. Mrs.
Tischler had gamely followed him out . . . While only
"Uncle" Martin engaged in the first part of his invitation,
Mrs. Tischler, who had a score of long standing to settle
with him, not only accepted a cigar from him and his
offer of a drink, but completely drained his flask before
handing it back.

One of the visiting outsiders, one of the girls from
the city, it appeared, could dance the Charleston, and
nothing would do but she just had to get up and show
how it was done. She could be excused for finally giving
in; she had been honest in her loud protestations that
she had only *seen* it done once or twice. No excuse
could be found for old Grandpa Leslie, on the other hand,
who had to get up and do *his* little dance . . . Grandpa,
who was sixty-eight, only a few years older than Mrs.
Tischler (she called him an old fool when he got out
on the floor) had been aging two or three years to everyone
else's one; his sons, daughters, grandsons and grand-
daughters were proudly exclaiming "and he's comin'
eighty" as he stumbled and hobbled around on the floor
like the imbecile he was. Pretending to be puffing and
that it was such hard work, he drank in the polite token
clap of applause that the good people of Minby had generously given him in the hopes that the old jackass would
go back to his seat. That, unfortunately, was just enough
to set him off once more, this time with one of his

grandsons to whom he had taught his little jig, "little Gordie," who was four past, almost five. But to even things out, the proud Leslie clan, eyes glistening, bragged that "little Gordie is on'y three . . ."

Two boxes above all had caught everybody's eye and they had been the subject of much animated discussion the whole evening. They held everyone's attention while the others were being bid on. Who had created this magnificent big battleship? And who had baked this mammoth Boston cream pie? Or was it a Boston cream cake? It wasn't really clear what it was, it wasn't a *box* in the usual sense. Word somehow had got around that it was a very special cake . . . And with all that whipped cream! And those tempting silver-colored candy spheres sprinkled tantalizingly all over, glistening like sequins!

Before they got around to auctioning the big boxes off, there was a bit of commotion caused by one of the smaller ones. The auctioneer had picked up one of the two white boxes with the green ribbon on it, and one of the boys had whispered to Old Jack Smythe that it belonged to Miss Johnstone the school teacher. This was right up Old Jack's alley! This was just the sort of thing he always waited for! What fun he was going to have, and he rubbed his hands in anticipation, chuckling as he ran the bidding up to a ridiculous figure.

The two old maids, Bertha and Daisy, had now been joined by Kerstin, and the three of them were whispering and giggling together! Could the box belong to one of them after all?

If Old Jack could boast about being the first one in every year with a load of grain, he would be able to boast after tonight how he had forced Mr. Mitchell the teacher up to the highest figure in Minby Box Social History . . .

Old Jack's wife, with her timorous little voice and her nervously gesticulating hands, was trying in vain to signal to him to quit his foolish bidding. He saw her, but he *didn't* see her, looked right past her as if she wasn't there. He was enjoying himself far, far too much! Christ, this was a real picnic, almost as much fun as one of his corn feeds! When Mr. Mitchell raised the bid fifty cents, Old Jack was in quick as a flash, no hesitation at all, to shoot the bid up a whole dollar.

Just as abruptly as the bidding started, just as abruptly now it stopped, there wasn't another sound. Old Jack's bid was the last. Mr. Mitchell quit bidding, and taking *señorita* Johnstone by the arm was going to call it an evening; they would have lunch down at Müllers' Hotel . . .

"What'sa matter, yuh tight-ass? Yuh broke?" snorted Old Jack as he tramped after the teachers making their way to the door. "By Jesus, I gets to eat with the lady, don't I?" And taking the box which he still hadn't paid for, he was going to claim Miss Johnstone for his supper partner.

"It's MY box, Jack," squeaked his wife, "I tried . . ."

"WHAT!" thundered old Smythe. "Why the hell didn't you tell me?" he roared, dropping his wife's box to the floor and jumping fairly and squarely on it with both feet.

Why didn't she tell him? this poor little browbeaten mouse of a woman who, the neighbors swore, didn't dare go to the privy without her husband's permission.

With mixed emotions too, Mr. Peyton retrieved his wife's battleship. He really thought it should have gone a lot higher, and he had been prepared to pay the price, by God! But when the other men saw him bid, they knew only too well whose box it was, and that he had already bid more than *his wife* could afford, since she was practically keeping the family. He promptly pulled out and lighted up the cigar that he had brought expressly for the occasion: he was going to show the people that smoke could actually be made to come out of *them* funnels!

And finally, at long last, the cake, this hour-long, nay evening-long conversationpiece, this Masterwork of the Culinary Arts, this . . . this . . . cake was set on a small table in the middle of the floor for all and sundry to admire. It shone there like a miniature white marble castle, the silvery candy spheres gleaming like sequins or magic casements under the glare of the artificial light. The Directors of the Agricultural Society had had a quick huddle and had decided, since this was such a special cake, they were going to try a special stunt. They had heard about it being done up at Missenden, why not here in little old Minby? Minby take a backseat to Missenden? They were going to set a special predetermined time; then, as the bids went higher and higher, each man would pay the amount by which he had increased the bid, and whoever made the last bid when the preset time was reached, would get to eat with the little lady whose dainty hands had prepared this *chef d'oeuvre*.

"Who'll be the first bidder?"

Old Catherwood, President of the Community Hall Board, set the reckless bidding tone by offering five dollars, an absolutely unheard-of opening bid in Minby. Why, most of the small boxes hadn't gone for a quarter of that ten minutes before! It was absolutely mad! But, with the gesture of a millionaire philanthropist in front of the klieg lights making a bequest of a thousand dollars, Mr. Catherwood plunked down the five dollars. Those same nasty tongues that start so many other stories, claim that he collected it back the next day out of the Community Hall funds . . .

And so the bidding went like fury, up fifty cents, up a dollar, up two dollars, higher, higher . . . Sixteen dollars, sixteen fifty . . . Twenty-two dollars . . . Wouldn't that damned alarm go off? Up another two bucks, higher, higher, forty-three . . . Forty-seven fifty . . . The excitement was at fever pitch when the gong sounded at long last. It had taken eight minutes and a half, and the final figure: *Fifty-six dollars!* When had anyone seen the likes in Minby before. The Lobb sisters would surely see that *that* got into *The Missenden Thunderbolt!*

Now — who had made this wonderful cake?

Blushing, Mrs. Catherwood, the wife of the President who had made that bold, opening five-dollar bid, bashfully got to her feet and, taking the knuckle of her thumb out of her mouth, coyly confirmed that her name was on the bottom of the pan. There were glances exchanged between some of Mrs. Catherwood's *friends* who knew that her reputation in the community was not based on her ability to cook, much less to bake an exhibition cake.

Angèle, our former hired girl, had worked for Mrs. Catherwood for part of one week years ago before coming to our place, a fact which she delighted in bringing to our attention again and again — and she declared that that had been enough for her. According to her, Mrs. Catherwood couldn't boil water without scorching it; her porridge in the mornings was so thin and watery one could swim in it, or, on the other hand, as thick and lumpy as a cold mutton stew. One thing she *could* do, Angèle, said, time and again, and that was "dirty more dishes than anyone else across the valley." Why she always had her table set with everything, "just like the pitchers in the magazines" Angèle added, "not just one knife, one fork and one spoon, but two, t'ree of each, *je vous assure*"; and serviettes, napkin rings, butter knives . . . Angèle liked what she called Mrs. Catherwood's *présentation,* she said it was very *chic,* but she pointed out that what she had to present was always underdone, overdone, or dried up to a frazzle, just fit to be thrown to the hogs.

This cake, *hélas,* followed the pattern of Mrs. Catherwood's other efforts. It was a gooey, gluey, heavy, indescribably sticky mass once one got under the cream on the outside, and Mr. Cantelon, the lucky winner, got his false plates stuck fast in it at the first mouthful. Oh, yes, he liked cake, he had assured Mrs. Catherwood seconds before taking the first bite, since he was sitting right beside her. He added, after he got his snappers apart and could talk again, that he was never much for midnight lunches.

To make sure her cake would be finished in time, Mrs. Catherwood had started on it early in the week. By the time it was finally decorated and brought into the hall and auctioned off, the thick layers of whipped cream had turned sour. So, as Mr. Cantelon with difficulty cut the cake into smaller portions, and generously started passing them around to the other people so "none of it would go to waste," or so the others "could have a sample of it too," knowing glances, I-told-you-so-looks with superior accompanying nods followed the Chairman of the Minby School Board around the hall as he distributed pieces of this fifty-six dollar culinary opus.

Jack Fender, who had recklessly put in a bid at the fifty-five dollar point, wiped his forehead when he thought of the narrow escape he'd had; he had worked for Catherwoods one week too when he first came out West and, echoing Angèle's sentiments, that had been enough for him too. He added, when he found out who had made the cake, that old Catherwood had been mighty careful not to "throw in another bid" after his grandstand opening gesture.

Twenty minutes after the furious bidding on her cake, Mrs. Catherwood's cheeks were still a faint pink from the excitement . . .

For the rest of the evening, under the benches, in the window sills, in empty overshoes, in overcoat pockets — no place was safe nor sacred — behind the piano, *in* the piano, in the dark recesses of the two cloakrooms, people were running into pieces of this colossal gastronomical disaster.

With the disguises removed, lunch about over, I was ready to go home when Dad said it was time for the likes of me to be in bed. I agreed.

What else could there have been after a night like that?

THE GIOCONDO SMILE

FIRST Mrs. Heppner's newborn baby passed away, but the doctor hadn't expected it to live anyway since it was two months premature; then a couple of days afterwards we heard that Grandma Soupley had died. No one was really surprised because she was over ninety and hadn't recovered from a nasty fall a few months previously.

"Gosh." Mom shivered. "Who'll be the third?"

At three o'clock in the afternoon, a whole hour ahead of coffee time, Mrs. Haugen came over to our place. She had just heard that Red Blaine had been gored by his bull out on the farm, and now she had seen Dr. Grenz driving through town "to beat sixty," probably heading for the Blaine place to see what he could do for the injured man. They recalled how that woman over at Cardston had been gored by a mad cow the year before, but she had been lucky enough to recover. Red, on the other hand, "was real bad!"

At three thirty the little Missenden ambulance came speeding through town in answer to Dr. Grenz's call, and at four o-clock it was back in Minby again, just in the nick of time to catch the passenger train for the city. Mr. Blaine had suffered such injuries, internal and external, that there was nothing our doctor could do for him with his limited facilities in Missenden.

The next afternoon Mom's premonitions came true. The doctors in the city hadn't been able to do anything for Red Blaine either. He died without regaining consciousness. The funeral would be Sunday afternoon at two o'clock from Bethel Tabernacle.

Now Mom wasn't the least bit happy that any one of these three people had died; but she had a macabre feeling of satisfaction nevertheless that *once again* she had been right.

Angèle Dempsey said out loud what probably three-quarters of Minby district people were thinking at that very moment: If a third person, or if anyone had to be gored, why couldn't it have been *Mrs.* Blaine instead of her husband? Violet Blaine, or Mrs. Red as she was more often called, was as universally feared and detested as Red had been loved and respected. She was viciously righteous and haughtily sanctimonious; she had an ice-pick-sharp tongue, the point of which most people in the community had felt. She practiced a kind of philosophy unique to herself. It went like this: Do unto others as most of the others would like to do unto you — but do it first! If she practiced biblical brotherhood relations, then it was in accordance with the unwritten rules of playful sibling rivalry that Cain and Abel followed. Truly, if she had lived at the appropriate moment in history, moving in the proper circles, she could have deposed Kings and unseated Emperors.

The most Violet Blaine could do in Minby was control Bethel Church Board and keep their ministers dancing. She ruled Bethel Ladies Aid with an iron hand; she *was* the Ladies Aid! She controlled the Minby Community Hall Board regardless of what Mr. Catherwood, the President, and the individual members of the board might think. She had incurred the wrath of Old Jack Smythe once when she scoffingly declared that no man — meaning Old Jack — who couldn't write his own name should be even considered as a member of the Minby Hall Board. At times, when she was particularly outraged and conducted herself accordingly, she was referred to — never to her face, of course — as "Violent" or "Violence" Blaine. Old Jack had vowed he'd get even with her.

Although he didn't publicize the running feud he had with her, neither did he really make any secret of it. He was biding his time. Like Angèle Dempsey . . . Indeed, Angèle felt she had every right to ask why it couldn't have been Mrs. Blaine instead of Red, for wasn't she still smarting from the spectacle Mrs. Red had made of her a couple of weeks before at the masquerade?

Mrs. Blaine wasn't in the habit of repeating the current scandal. No — she stored it, compartmentalized and catalogued it, and when it suited her purpose, she would dig up long-forgotten facts and throw a whole sheaf of them in a person's face at the most inopportune time. Nothing was sacred. Only she and hers seemed to be immune; no one, it appeared, had anything on her. If she was as impregnable a fortress *before* she was married as she appeared to be *now,* twenty years after, then nothing with the slightest tinge of believable scandal could have occurred or been concocted in connection with her. She *must* have looked *then* as she did now. Being married to Red Blaine for twenty years couldn't have done *that* to her. . .

The second last minister Bethel had, one who had served as missionary in the Fiji Islands, found her just too much to cope with and preferred, since he was going to lose his scalp anyway, to go back to the headhunters in the jungles . . . The first week he was in Minby, he had innocently lit up his meerschaum pipe down at the Post Office while waiting for his mail, and Mrs. Blaine had seen him. He was smoking his pipe, his favorite pipe, one he was wont to caress as he filled it, in exactly the same way he had been smoking and caressing his meerschaum pipe for thirty years. He was told that the Bethel pastors didn't smoke pipes, they didn't smoke anything!

For the first month, this same Reverend Keynes, fearfully but happily smoking his favorite meerschaum, played a weekly game of billiards, *not* a vulgar game of snooker or pool, but *billiards*, an English gentleman's game, he said . . . Mrs. Blaine heard about this dissipation and he was informed that Bethel pastors, when they entered the Minby Pool Room and Barber Shop, did so for a haircut or shave; they didn't play pool, nor did they dally once their hair had been cut. Reverend Keynes would be well advised furthermore, to get his haircut in Missenden when he preached up there, she said, because the Barber Shop in that town had no Pool Room in conjunction with it.

The first month too, Reverend Keynes, an ex-service chaplain, innocently joined the Missenden Branch of the Canadian Legion and attended the special meeting they held to finalize their plans to welcome the Governor General, Viscount Willingdon. When word was as usual relayed to the Blaine farm that Reverend Keynes had been seen *with a bottle of Old Horn beer in his hand,* she thought the matter of sufficient gravity to call a special meeting of the Bethel Church Board. Mrs. Blaine had been *shocked* . . . If Reverend Keynes had not signed a two-year contract, it was common knowledge that he would have left before his time was up. "Violent" Blaine had threatened not only to leave the church, but to take a good part of the congregation with her.

Mrs. Blaine was as belligerently bold and crassly highhanded when she settled her other little community affairs. When Mrs. Steiner, long-time housekeeper for one of the bachelors, put on a dinner and shower for her only daughter and future son-in-law, it was an invitational affair, and she had signed the cards "Mrs. Alfreda Steiner." Mrs. Red, evidently the only other person in Minby in on the secret, chose that moment to scornfully drop her bomb and say, with her well-oiled smile of derision:

"*Mrs.* Steiner, my foot — she's never been married!"

Unfortunately it was true, Alfreda had never married. Whatever score Mrs. Blaine had had to settle with Alfreda, she was prepared to do so without one moment's consideration for the innocent daughter or the daughter's husband-to-be.

For twenty years then, Mrs. Red had been putting crosses over the uncrossed *t's,* dotting any undotted *i's,* keeping the records straight as she probably would have said. A more maliciously evil-minded, piously powerful female wasn't to be found in Minby, Missenden or Culbertson. Had Old Jack Smythe met his match in this vicious termagant?

I was just one of the dozen idlers at the station when the one o'clock train pulled in. We all saw the rough box that contained Mr. Blaine's coffin unloaded from the baggage car. It had been shipped by the undertaker from the city that morning. It was transferred immediately to the waiting truck and the coffin brought directly into Bethel Tabernacle for the funeral to be held less than an hour later.

Mrs. Blaine and red-haired Christina, both dressed in mourning, got off from the first passenger coach. Mrs. Blaine played the part of the bereaved widow to perfection, heavily veiled, shrouded in black, black hat, black gloves, black purse, black everything, leaning heavily on her daughter. She looked neither right nor left, walking slowly, consciously striving to add to the solemn picture of tragic sorrow she was sure she presented. She and Christina, her and Red's only child, had both followed Mr. Blaine to the hospital when he was taken to the city a few days before, and had accompanied the body back home again; now they were being met by Hedley Cantelon, Mrs. Blaine's brother, and driven over to the big Lobb house where they would wait out the hour until it was time for the service to start.

What Mrs. Red didn't see, but what everyone else at the station did see only a minute later, was another woman dressed in black, accompanied as Mrs. Blaine had been by a red-haired girl, as fiery a red as Christina's hair, as fiery a red as Red Blaine's hair had been. This girl might have been two or three years older than Christina, she could just as well have been a year or two younger . . . No one at the Minby station knew who they were. They had got off from the next car to the one occupied by Mrs. Blaine and her daughter. They were met by no one; they went directly to the waiting room of the station where they remained until about twenty minutes to two, making appropriate use of their handkerchiefs all the while, then they, too, went to the church.

Little Bethel Tabernacle was jam-packed, with another hundred, mostly men, standing out in the church yard paying their last respects to Red Blaine.

Angèle Dempsey was at the funeral too, of course, and saw these two strange women in black. Although she *as always* had her seat up near the front, she could nevertheless recite pew by pew all those who had been present at a funeral within the church. Angèle wouldn't miss a funeral for all the world — she'd sooner go to a real sad burial any day than to a movie with Mary Pickford. On more than one occasion when she was still working for us she had gone up to Missenden *between trains* to attend funerals of people she scarcely knew. When Dad's papers came each day, she would leave off drying the dishes and pick up the *Tribune* for a few minutes, since it, so she said, had the *loveliest* obituaries of all . . . She was disappointed at any funeral, however, when they didn't open the coffin. She wasn't disappointed in Bethel today, the coffin was opened, and anyone wishing to pay their respects (or who wanted to see what a man looked like who had been gored by a bull) could have a last look at Mr. Blaine.

Angèle's curiosity had been at fever pitch, for had she ever seen such a corpse before? and hadn't she heard on very good authority that Red had been gored "just something awful"? She was happy to report to my mother afterwards that Red had made a *fine* corpse nevertheless.

When Angèle filed past the coffin, she followed hard on the heels of the two mysterious women in black.

"They bent real low over Mr. Blaine," she told Mom, lingering over the dramatic details. "You just shoulda seen the look on old 'Violent' Blaine's face when she saw them, especially when she had a look at the girl!"

The chief mourners, of course, were in the first rows, directly in front of the coffin, and the people filing past had to go between them and the coffin. Angèle had observed everything very carefully. She was beside herself with curiosity after the funeral, however. So was Mrs. Haugen when the two of them came over to our place for four o'clock coffee. There were certain details that neither Angèle nor Mrs. Haugen had quite sorted out. Perhaps between the two of them. . .

If Angèle and Mrs. Haugen were curious, Mrs. Blaine must have been dumfounded by the unexpected appearance of these strange women at *her* Red's funeral. She no doubt thought that she, the sorrowing widow, would speak with them in the grave yard, at the grave side, when they approached to extend their sympathy, when she could *receive* them individually.

"Yes," Mrs. Blaine was assured, "they got into a car" — she could never find out whose — "and they went out to the cemetery!"

"No," contradicted another, "they didn't go to the cemetery at all, they got a ride all right, but they turned the other way at Müller's Hotel — they *prob'ly* went

around to the station to wait for the four o'clock back
to the city!''

There the trail ended as mysteriously as it had begun
— for if one could count on a good handful of people
at the one o'clock train, there were never more than
two or three for the one going back at four. Today, probably on account of the funeral, there hadn't been a soul.

By nightfall these two women had become the subject
of conversation in the whole Minby district! Little stories
began to circulate, each new rumor being a little spicier
than the last one, all eventually finding their way out
to the Blaine farm and Mrs. Blaine who, understandably,
was in a rage. Lornie Cantelon, her own nephew, was
saying how furious she was for having ordered that fifteen
hundred dollar casket.

Mr. Blaine would have been flattered by some of
the tales that had set little old Minby rocking. Indeed
some of the stories of his prowess, now posthumously
related, would have made him smile in his coffin — in
spite of lacerations to his head and neck, a broken pelvis
and a crushed rib cage.

"The gay dog!'' said Mrs. Tischler with that glint
in her eye. "I *allus* said 'Still waters run deep.' ''

"Guschlbaur and Martin Eriksson must'a ben beginners alongside him,'' said Mrs. Clarke, reminiscing
speculatively.

Old Jack Smythe winked slyly at every new story
that made the rounds. Was it because as long as they
were talking about Red they weren't talking about him?

A couple of weeks after the funeral, with the excitement subsided and Minby once more back to its prosaic
normal, Old Jack, eyes sparkling, told me, really confiden-
tially this time, that he'd let me in on a big story when
I got a little older.

"A humdinger, Wally,'' he added.

But I had already caught on.

"KASS"KOMOS'S FIRST PHONOGRAPH

I REMEMBER the winter my Dad built our first radio. I recall too, somewhat later, when we got our first radio with a loud speaker — it was an earlier model of the Atwater-Kent we now had. Perhaps the most vivid memory of all was the big day we got our brand-new Heintzman piano. Although I can remember with great clarity these Viggo musical landmarks, I can't remember when we got the little old Edison phonograph — we always had it, and it had the undisputed place of honor in the living room until displaced by the Atwater-Kent. Our musical selections were limited to the forty-odd cylinder records, stuffed in their orange-colored protective cardboard rolls, stacked like cordwood on a shelf beneath the machine.

My Dad's all-time favorite musician was Harry Lauder, and since he did the buying there were several of his recordings. And when he was heard to whistle, it was generally "Oh, it's nice to get up in the morning." In fact, Dad was such a Harry Lauder fanatic that he dropped everything to go to hear him when he toured Canada, making just about as many preparations for that trip to the city as he did for his trip to Sweden. No other living human being, not even the Prince of Wales on his epoch-making journey to Canada to visit his ranch, would have made my father undertake that trip.

I played all our records, even the two or three hymns . . . That was, of course, before Reverend Kreuz arrived. They were seldom played, however, usually on Sunday. The "church" records probably came with the machine or Dad or Mom (most likely Mom) included them because it was the thing to do, concrete and audible proof that the Viggos constituted a respectable Christian household. I always ended up with the same favorites. One of them I had played so often and handled so much that I wore away the title on the end of the cylinder. It was a mandolin orchestra. One of the Minby farmers many miles south of town, evidently a great admirer of this instrument, happened into our house one day when this record was playing. For several years thereafter on his weekly trips in to the village he would make a special call at our house and ask my mother to put that record on for him! When she did, he would listen, hands folded piously; tears would come to his eyes, he would get all choked up and generally say it was "just like a dream" and go, but not before he had given each of us kids a nickel or a chocolate bar.

Sometimes my favorite was "Silver Bell," sometimes it was the "Mocking Bird," but most often it was the "Bell in the Lighthouse." Each of these records had its little specialty that had captivated me and held my interest from my earliest years. "Silver Bell" had a history all its own, one Angèle used to recount. This particular recording had "Home Sweet Home" running softly through the background of the title piece, very much like an unemphasized obbligato. I can remember as a small tot feeling that there was *something else* going on beside "Silver Bell"; I would follow along the thread of the other melody for a few bars and lose it as it elusively merged with the voice.

I could never quite grasp what it was about this obbligato that intrigued me until one day, according to Mom and Angèle, I came to them with eyes as big as saucers, so excited I could hardly talk: I had made the discovery that two pieces were being played at the same time! In my excitement all I could do was pull them out to the other room to show them my discovery. I played it by the hour thereafter when I was big enough to operate the machine alone. Angèle said it was the happiest day of her life when the new Atwater-Kent radio took up its position in the living room and the old Edison was banished upstairs.

As for the "Mocking Bird," could I hear it today with the same pleasure? Probably not; but for me as a youngster, the man who imitated the bird calls had my unqualified admiration. For a long time I thought the singer was dreaming about Swee Talley, and I had a confused idea that Swee could have been an Indian name like Cree, undoubtedly because of my association with "Silver Bell," since I could never play the one record without sooner or later putting the other on. I knew the voice of the mocking bird was an imitation, and I would put it on over and over again until Angèle, finally driven to desperation, would stop the machine, slam the lid shut, and tell me to go out in the yard and play "for heaven's sakes."

But oh the last record, the "Bell in the Lighthouse" . . . I had built up a whole mythology around this which involved the Inchcape Rock, my mother's Swedish Bible, and the story of one of the early English Kings who had never smiled again because of his children who had been lost at sea.

It must have been a Danish King, and his children were probably on a trip over to Denmark. I don't know the name of the artist — that was technical information of absolutely no consequence at the time. Certainly one of the greats of his day, the big selling point of the record was this singer's masterful handling of the bass, although the concluding stanza where that was most featured, was the part I cared for least. He would have been very vexed had he known I generally left that out. I missed whole lines of the lyrics as the record scratched along, one spot in particular which I could never quite understand.

Sometimes it sounded like "and over the sea go I", and others like "and over the seagulls high" . . .

I loved to hear "When the bell in the lighthouse rings ding dong," for it seemed to be ringing in the *dark* and I could hear it coming in to me over the waves. It was beautiful. In the background again was a beautiful obbligato that sent shivers up and down my spine, perhaps a muted violin. Associated with the lighthouse, the Inchcape Rock and the princes who had drowned, was this sepia-colored print from the Creation in Mom's old Swedish Bible, showing the earth before the waters and land were divided. The *light* house, by definition, should have been the central point of concentrated illumination, but my memories of this record, strangely enough, leave me with much the opposite impression. I used to select just the parts I wanted to hear, playing them over and over again so often that had the machine not been given away, the needle would have cut the cylinder in two. Yes, alas, the old Edison was given away this day, and I had to hand part of its trappings over to the new owner. It came about this way.

A few years earlier Kass Komoschewski with his wife and three or four kiddies showed up in Minby out of nowhere. Komoschewski was the name we read on his cream can when he shipped any cream. His first name was either Kasimir or Kasper and this everyone shortened to "Kass" just like his foot-long family name was later officially emasculated to Komos. That occurred when he came home from a term in jail . . .

Kass spoke Russian and German, but not one word of English when we first knew him. His wife, on the contrary, soon spoke flawless English along with the other languages she already knew. She was brilliant; her husband was intelligent too, but as long as she could do the talking for them he didn't see the necessity of acquiring the *lingua franca* of Minby.

Kass, of course, was by no means unique in this respect. There were several heads of families who had had to learn some English to get along those first years; but once the children were old enough to talk and interpret, they would do the talking for the parents, who remained in the background and made their wishes known and the old folks were seldom heard to speak English again.

Kass Komos had homesteaded on a quarter, as had so many of his compatriots. Unlike the majority of them, he didn't make a success of it. He worked like a slave, but could never acquire enough equipment to get going. Where others could get credit, Kass could get none, although he didn't owe a cent to anyone. Against him was his unprepossessing appearance plus his inability to speak English. He couldn't talk business with anyone, and the machine agents and some of the other merchants just didn't like to deal through a woman.

Often when he should have been home doing his own work, Kass was giving a hand elsewhere to earn a little cash. He did most of the killing for Mr. Kovacz when he butchered, and plucked thousands of chickens for him too. To get even more cash in a hurry, he was persuaded to set up a still by one of his smart-talking Russian country men. Things flourished exceedingly well for a while, Kass had ready money for a change, but he was the one accused of bootlegging, the one to be sentenced to jail.

That was the beginning of the end. How his wife was able to hang on to the little they had was a mystery, with several young children, two of school age and another born while the father was in jail. She didn't get much help from the people around Minby, she rather bothered them . . . The Minby people made their charitable donations anonymously (anonymously as far as the recipient was concerned) to the missions in Africa or China.

By the time Kass was out of jail and home again, he had learned a smattering of English. Thereafter he referred to his term in jail as his "trouble," never making any bones about having spent two years behind bars.

Kass and his family were now squatting on the good-for-nothing Pringle place just a short distance out of Minby and from here he would walk into town each day looking for work. It was the same farm where the LaRocques had found refuge.

Mr. Komos had had difficulty before he was sent to prison trying to get work; now with his somewhat damaged reputation it was even more difficult. To my knowledge only my Dad and Mr. Kovacz would have him around, yet my Dad said he was worth any two men. Indeed, Kass had been the victim of circumstances and of a smart, fast-talking bootlegger who should have been jailed too. My Dad was convinced that there wasn't a more reliable, honest, hard-working man in the Minby district, given the chance. So, for several weeks Kass Komos would be at the shop door, waiting for Dad to open up. If my Dad was up early (this in the winter) Mr. Komos must have been up an hour earlier to get into Minby and at the shop ahead of him. He swung the big sledge hammer tirelessly hour after hour as he and my Dad filled huge gunny sacks with plow points. If they weren't used this year, Dad would say, he would have them on hand for the next, or for the next after that. In short, making plow points was the pretext for giving Mr. Komos something to do.

I had come to regard the old Edison phonograph as my own personal property. Who else but me ever played it any more? The big, dark, windowless, stuffy clothes closet upstairs had become my private Music Hall and in it I had installed the little machine on top of Dad's old steamer trunk. There was a twenty years' accumulation of old shoes on the floor, another twenty years' accumulation of old clothes on the hooks lining the walls. When I organized my little concerts, I didn't disturb anyone; how could anyone hear me from the living room or kitchen below?

But my Dad must have heard me playing the little Edison one day at coffee time, otherwise he wouldn't have thought of the old phonograph. It had, at that time, been out of sight for several years. My father's thoughts probably went like this:

"Poor Mr. Komos — he gets no pleasure out of life; he's spent the past two years in jail; he has nothing but the bare walls of the Pringle shack to look at, and that must be just like a jail. He doesn't get a paper, he can't read, he hasn't got a radio . . . Why don't we just give him the phonograph?"

So he asked Mr. Komos whom he had invited into the house for four o'clock coffee, and who was now sitting uncomfortably on the edge of his chair, if he wanted the machine. According to Mom, Mr. Komos didn't seem to grasp what a phonograph was. And wasn't it just possible that *he had never seen one before?* The first I knew of my father's generous intention, was when he came upstairs to get it.

When Dad told me whom he was going to give the old Edison to, I thought he had gone out of his mind. My brain, surprisingly enough, functioned quick enough to get in one question. It was hitting beneath the belt, I know:

"But Mr. Komos can hardly speak English — Do you think he'll understand Harry Lauder?"

But Dad was to be neither swayed nor swerved from his purpose by so devious and underhanded an argument. He hesitated, it's true, but not for more than a few seconds; he already had the phonograph under his arm.

"Wally, you bring down the records!"

As I did, I felt as if I were carrying flowers to my own funeral.

I was unconsolable for several days. Both Dad and Mom said I was carrying on like a big baby and that I would get over it. I did. Not too long after I learned that if I could no longer enjoy the music the little Edison produced, neither would anyone else.

OF WAR AND PEACE

THE LAST "Entrance" examination, besides marking
the end of the school year for me, marked the end of a
declared truce between my cousin Blaine on the one hand,
and Vic Armstrong, on the other. For many weeks past
there had been really bad blood between them; tales had
been circulated too, some of which they may have contributed to themselves. Their feelings of animosity
reached such a pitch about a week before the examinations that it was mutually agreed that they were going
"to have it out" at four o'clock when the last test was
over.

Although Blaine was my cousin, I was to be Vic
Armstrong's second. Why? Only because Vic had asked
me first. Erik Haugen was to act in the same capacity
for Blaine. There would be no other witnesses; no one
else knew that today this question was going to be finally
settled.

This was the most ridiculous scrap on record. We
had decided weeks before that the fight — it was definitely
going to be a battle to the finish! — was to take place
behind the old Livery Barn. Perhaps the most incongru-
ous aspect of this quarrel was the fact that the four of
us, the two adversaries and their seconds, arrived on
the field of battle at the same time. Instead of meeting
there, we were practically walking arm in arm the last
hundred yards. And one would have thought, too, from
our animated conversation that we were discussing the
latest talkie, the big ball tournament that was coming,
or the exam just over. What was being decided with so
much fervor was how the fight should be conducted.
Anything, almost, save the use of a lethal weapon, was

to be permitted and it would only stop when one or the other gave up. Or worse. . .

"What are you guys fighting for anyway?" I asked.

"Ask *him!*" said Blaine belligerently, indicating Vic with a nod of his head in that direction.

"Yuh mean, *ast him!*" said Vic, with a funny forced laugh, pointing right back at Blaine again.

"Yes," said Erik, and the role of mediator seemed to fit him much better than it did me, because he quite frequently associated with the two of them, certainly more than I did. "We know you're going to have it out; we know that the best man'll win, but what's it all going to settle? What are you guys fighting about *anyways?*"

"He started it," said Blaine defiantly.

"The hell I did, you did, goddam it!" snorted Vic.

"Started W H A T ?" asked both Erik and I together, once again seizing our chance to try to get to the root of the matter.

"He knows damned well!" said Vic pointing vaguely in Blaine's direction.

"So does he," retorted Blaine.

Both Vic and Blaine appeared to be eager to start battle. But wasn't there a certain amount of bravado in all that? Once when I was in Missenden with Dad we saw a couple of dogs on leashes straining at each other, only a couple of feet apart, growling savagely, baring their teeth, the hair on their necks rising; and two minutes later we saw the same two dogs run yelping off in opposite directions when they were let go . . . Would Blaine or Vic, or would *both* of them back down at the last moment when we finally gave them the signal to start fighting? It didn't look like it.

They were squaring off now. Vic hesitated and finally took off his glasses and handed them to me, thereby putting himself at a decided disadvantage; he couldn't leave them on, he didn't have five cents with which to

buy a new pair and if these got broken his mother would
have to pay for new ones. Vic wasn't trying to sneak
out of the fight by making it look that it was going to
be one-sided in Blaine's favor.

Now they were shaking hands! I didn't know people
did that sort of thing before a fight. Why should they
shake hands? How in Sam Hill did Vic or Blaine know
they should start off this way?

Then it started!

Impossible to say who got in the first blow. There
was one sickening thud after the other of fist against flesh,
followed by an occasional grunt as a healthy blow struck
home. Never a cry nor a sound of complaint came from
either of the battlers. They were on their feet, then they
were down on the ground, the one on his back with the
other on top appearing to have the advantage — but only
for a moment; a quick half-turn and the roles were
instantly reversed . . .

And so it went on for five minutes, ten minutes,
fifteen . . . Erik and I gazed horrified when the blood
started to flow, the one with a gash over the eye, the
other with a bloody nose.

"For God's sake, stop!" I shouted.

By a miracle they both stopped, a foot from each
other, hands raised protectively, gasping for air, heads
at exactly the same height like two fighting cocks, gazing
into each other's eyes, trying to divine the next motion
to be made by the opponent. First one smiled hesitantly,
then the other.

"Had enough?" asked Vic.

"Nope. Have you?" asked Blaine.

"No . . . But don't you think we should rest for
a few minutes till we get our breath?" asked Vic.

"Okay, just time for a quick smoke!"

"What's it all about *anyways?*" asked Erik, appalled
at the prospect of this senseless slaughter starting all

over again. He was just about ready to burst into tears from this show of foolish stupid brutality.

"Do you know what started it all in the first place?" I asked. "Does either of you know what it's all about?"

"He knows damned well!" said Vic blowing a big cloud of smoke at Blaine, handing him the cigaret he had just rolled and lit so *he* could have a puff.

"So does he!" replied Blaine just as energetically as he took the proffered cigaret.

It seemed that that was just about where we four had all come in twenty-five minutes earlier. Was it really and truly going to start all over again? It was, because at the end of five minutes, at the end of their cigaret, when they decided they had rested enough they shook hands once more and started in again.

"What the hell *are* we fighting for?" asked Vic, dodging a right from Blaine but getting a cracking good one in of his own.

"Didn't *you* goddam well start it?" asked Blaine.

"Start what?" asked Vic. "Christ, that one you give me on the cheek hurt like a bastard!"

"You wasn't exactly passin' out love taps neither!" said Blaine. "Look at your bloody knuckles!"

And while they stopped to admire each other's bruises — for when they admired each other's injuries weren't they admiring how hard *they* themselves had hit? — I once again suggested that since it wasn't clear to anybody who had started what, and since the one was as good a *man* as the other, why didn't we just go around to the pump and wash up and call it quits?"

"You game, Vic?" "I am if you are!"

"Okay, put 'er there!"

And laughing at their bravery, or was it to cover up their feeling of foolishness, or was it simply relief to have the air finally cleared, they shook hands again.

They were friends once more.

OF AIR MAIL AND BEACONS

H AD it not been my lot to be Vic's second, I would
never have followed him home after the fight the same
evening, nor would I have seen what I was fated to see —
I just wasn't that close a friend of his. About the closest
I had to a steady friend was Erik Haugen, and he was so
exasperating — or perhaps I was the one at fault — that
even we weren't on speaking terms three quarters of the
time. Vic told me that I just had to go the rest of the way
home with him to his grandmother's to see his beacon, it
would only take another fifteen minutes.

What, exactly, was a beacon? I didn't know except
that for some time now on good nights we had been
seeing the beam of the brand new one about twenty miles
east of Minby when it flashed its light. It had been set
up for the newly inaugurated air service. I had in my
album the brand new 1928 five-cent Air Mail stamp which
Dad had given me as a surprise a year and a half before
but I still hadn't seen a mail plane. Last year, last July
as a matter of fact, the Western Canada Airways plane
had flown right over Minby on its epoch-making flight
from Vancouver to Winnipeg, making the trip in *just
under twelve hours*. But our confirmation class had been
out at the lake all that month and two weeks more, so
I missed that. This year Lethbridge had in fact become
a crossroads. It had already been on the line connecting
Edmonton with the points south in Montana, and now
there was this new line east and west with a strong likeli-
hood of it expanding *still more*.

Vic was explaining to me that he had this turntable
that kept on going round and around, and mounted on
a platform just like a real beacon was this light that flashed

in a circle . . . He'd let me see it, he'd even let me start it and stop it.

Of course I was interested in anything that smacked of motors, Meccano sets, toy steam engines, mechanics in general, and we were doing the last two hundred yards to his grandmother's at a slow gallop. When we got to the house he told me I had to wait outside while he fixed things up a little. It had to be a surprise.

First of all he had to run into the house for props and I could hear his grandmother give him the dickens for the mess he was in because of the fight. He came out seconds later with a candle, matches and some string and headed for the little shack beside the house which served as their wood and coal shed. Once more I had to stay outside. The door closed behind him and after a minute's preparation he pulled the blind down over the one window. It was thus totally dark inside when he drew the door shut after calling me in.

There in the darkness in front of me all I could see was this jam tin turned upside down on the revolving platform with an inch and a half hole cut out of the side with the tin snips, and a feeble light coming out of it. As it turned and when the hole faced me, I could see the lighted candle inside the tin, and I could hear some sort of motor humming softly away. That was sweet m-u-s-i-c to Vic's ears. That was the beacon . . . Of course I was surprised and impressed at the effectiveness of this rudimentary machine although it really didn't *flash,* but would I spoil Vic's fun by telling him that? For him the illusion was absolutely complete, probably better than the real one out in the country, even if this one, his, was only o-n-e candle-power.

"Gotta save the candle, I on'y got this'n left," he said, letting up the blind and throwing open the door.

With daylight streaming in again I had ample chance to examine his handiwork more closely.

"Where did you get the motor?" I asked uneasily.

"Out at the 'Old Pringle Place!' " he said enthusiastically, as if the unexpected source of the motive power and how he had chanced upon it should add even more to my pleasure in seeing it.

"The 'Old Pringle Place!' "

That horrible suspicion was fast being confirmed . . . That was the good-for-nothing quarter just outside of Minby; that was where LaRocques had squatted until last Christmas when they just up and left; that was where Kass Komos had squatted with his wife and kids after his release from jail. Was this *my* phonograph? Rather had this beacon *been* my phonograph? It had . . .

Vic had been out to the "Old Pringle Place" snooping around right after Kass and his family moved out. What Mr. Komos couldn't pile on to his one wagon or what he or his wife regarded as useless they had simply left behind. My phonograph which I had prized above all else in the world was probably the first thing they discarded when they loaded up. Had they *ever* played it? Had Mr. Komos even understood what Dad so generously offered him that day?

"What did you do with the records?" I asked when I felt I could talk without my voice trembling too much.

What a question to ask! Here was the little phonograph stripped of everything but the motor, it didn't even *look* like a gramophone. The little governor was set to turn the "beacon" as slowly as possible, there was no sign of the speaker anywhere, no sign of the cylinder or pickup. Vic had even had to knock off the lid of the cabinet to make room for his rotating platform . . .

Without waiting for his answer to my question, I was out of the shack and heading for home. Neither he nor Blaine had flinched or shed a tear as they took and gave blow for blow only an hour before. I couldn't let him see my face now.

EPILOGUE

It wasn't long after I finished Grade Eleven that we left Minby. That was in the early thirties. Dad, who never said "dash" nor "darn," let alone "damn," could never bring himself to refer to these years as the "dirty thirties" as everyone else did. For him they were the "bad years." How my Dad could just up and leave everything he owned after almost three decades of tireless activity is understandable only to those who lived through those desolate years themselves and who abandoned — or who were tempted to abandon — their farms or businesses as he did. Some young people commenting on the film *The Drylanders* which described this period, remarked, "It couldn't have been as bad as all that — the film producers are exaggerating once more . . ." Alas, it was only too true. A short poem by Fred Laight* summarizes this period in prairie history all too well:

Soliloquy

I have seen tall chimneys without smoke,
  And I have seen blank windows without blinds,
  And great dead wheels, and motors without minds,
And vacant doorways grinning at the joke.

I have seen loaded wagons creak and sway
  Along the roads into the North and East,
  Each dragged by some great-eyed and starving beast
To God knows where, but just away — away.

*quoted with the generous consent of the author.

> And I have heard the wind awake at nights
> Like some poor mother left with empty hands,
> Go whimpering in the silent stubble lands
> And creeping through bare houses without lights.
>
> These comforts only have I for my pain —
> The frantic laws of statesmen bowed with cares
> To feed me, and the slow, pathetic prayers
> Of godly men that somehow it shall rain.

Dad went back to Minby on one occasion when his old pioneer friend Mr. Gottselig died, and he spent a few days visiting in the district then. That was enough for him . . . Even if things were once more back to normal, perhaps even booming, he was glad he moved to the Okanagan when he did. He marveled at the sequence of events that had brought him to Minby in the first place, but he marveled even more that he had stuck it so long, even in the so-called "good times." He should have had a lesson from that first homestead he was on. Minby, of course, was all right when it rained and when things grew, but the hard, months-long winters and the infernally hot dry summers were too much to put up with, especially for one who enjoyed seeing things fresh and green. Dad was much happier now where he was. He was getting older and that could also have made a difference.

When Dad left Minby, eight Viggos left; and almost twenty more —*farbror* Hasse's big family and their first grandchildren — only a couple of months after, once my father was settled in British Columbia and had found a place for them too. It was the appropriate move for Uncle Hasse and Aunt Birgitt. That made an irreparable dint in the population of the old village, quite apart from the other families that had already begun the exodus.

Could they, could my Dad, be blamed for leaving what looked like certain bankruptcy?

Could I only have been in Minby at the turn of the century from the very beginning, to make a historical record of exactly who and what came first, and then of exactly who left the district and why. It still intrigues me to think about the *first* man who came and said "This is the place" or "This will be Minby." Who was he? Minby's decline and fall can be observed in all its phases in any of the dozens of Alberta, Manitoba and Saskatchewan villages and towns that are drying up and disappearing just as my village did. Minby was doomed from the beginning, like these others are, but it just happened to be among the first to go. And think of other names that are as good as gone from the prairie map, all of which had their little day. Huge cities with hundreds of thousands like Babylon, and other great centers like Baalbek, Nineveh and Carthage come and go, why not villages and towns with only a few hundreds? In three years, from 1965 to 1968, no less than 132 Post Offices were shut down in Alberta! What's the difference, really, if it is only thirty or forty years instead of three centuries, or three thousand years? A way of life evidently can't be fixed once and for all, certainly not in *our* day when one technological change coming fast upon the heels of another is accompanied by corresponding changes that influence every facet of our economic life. Before World War I no one, you might say, had a car in Minby. If the first automobiles were rare and expensive then, and if the roads were terrible, well nigh impassable at times, no one would have predicted that by 1930, in less than two decades, everybody would be driving a vehicle of some kind, unless, like Old Scott McEachern he refused to have one. A lot had a second car, or a truck in reserve. Indeed, Model T's were given away or sold for as little as twenty dollars in the early thirties.

Arendson's store closed up when we left. Maynard's had almost gone up in flames a few years before that, the same night that Belette's elevator burned down. Arendson was a man who couldn't say "no" to his customers and most of them took advantage of him, just as they had taken advantage of Einar Haugen before him. He couldn't pay the wholesalers with the worthless promissory notes he got from the farmers, prominent among whom was Hedley Cantelon, chairman of the Minby School Board. That still left Mr. Kovacz's store for a while. Mr. Kovacz had more in common with Old Scott McEachern than first met the eye. Like Old Scott, Mr. Kovacz, although of the community, was never really a part of it either, because he wasn't a Christian — although Einar Haugen said on many an occasion that he was a better Christian than a lot of them in Minby. Old Scott *was* a Christian, but not the good, well-dressed, car-driving, debt-ridden kind. However, Mr. Kovacz was no more to be criticized for wanting his children to marry other Jews than the Schurks for wanting their children to marry other Protestants and the Murphys, other Catholics. Seeing no suitable suitors for his many daughters in Minby *or* Missenden, *or* Culbertson, *or* Rottingdean, Mr. Kovacz started business all over again in the city. That left *no* stores in Minby where once we had four! For a while Mr. Roberts in the garage kept a few loaves of bread on hand, along with confectionery and tobacco "just to oblige . . ."

I was back on leave the first time in the early forties. The Commonwealth Air Training Scheme had a base not too far from Griswold, and I was able to get down to the old home town a couple of times on a "forty-eight." After all it was only a few stations away. I was amazed at the evolution, revolution, deterioration or degeneration (call it what you will!) that had taken place in the ten years I had been away. I had left fruit-growing country to go into the Air Force. It was inevitable, when I came back to the birthplace I had left as an early teenager, that I would see everything through different eyes. I remembered things of course as they were when I was considerably younger and that makes a difference. The Old Stone School which had always looked so big and massive, even though it had only one room, now just looked like an empty country school — a bit larger perhaps — it wasn't used for anything. When I came back the second time, it was nowhere to be seen! It was as if an old friend had died and been cremated. And isn't that just about what happened? The two rooms of the "new" school were more than enough to accommodate the pupils and when it was clear that the old one would never be required again, it was first of all burned out, then literally blown up and dumped into its own basement, the ground smoothed over _exactly_ as it had been forty years before. No doubt empty buildings with boarded-over windows _are_ unsightly . . . Yet for twenty-five years that old school had tied all the human threads from six to sixteen together, just like the village of Minby itself did all the human relationships for miles around, regardless of age. Now bigger school units were the rule and the Minby school kids in the higher grades were being bussed up to Missenden. The few people left in Minby wrung their hands once more when this happened and said, "This is the end!" They had been singing this same lamentation like Job for a good many years, but the voices in the choir were getting fewer and fewer as time went by.

I spent the night at Gottselig's farm. Where else would I have gone? Magdalena, Theresa's older sister, and I spent the evening going through her old snapshots. She had hundreds of them and I was present in many when I was only a babe in arms. There were others when I was two years old, three, four and so on up till the very year we left. I could have spent days drooling over those albums renewing acquaintances of people whose common denominator that particular day had been their love and respect for the friendly Gottselig family they had come to visit. I could recognize my parents in the early snaps, and quite a few of the other adults, but not many of the children — perhaps because the older people changed relatively little, and we younger ones quite a lot.

Magdalena had never married — she had stayed at home to look after her father and her brothers after her mother had dropped dead the year of our farcical Entrance exams and she had no family of her own. The kids in those pictures whose faces she knew by heart constituted her enormous brood. She had dozens of snaps of our family that even we didn't have, many of which she let me keep. She knew she was making me a gift I couldn't have bought at any price.

"Boy! I wish I had a dime for every time I clicked that old Kodak!" she said with a chuckle.

It was interesting to confront a handful of pictures on a given theme. If I had wanted to, for instance, I could have gathered a sizable pile together around the Viggo family; or another on the evolution of the automobile, because cars were included as a backdrop in almost all the pictures. Magdalena smiled over the selection she assembled to show what the smart young Minby "flapper" was wearing. Being a good seamstress she had reason to recall those tomboy skirts and jazz garters which she had made up for herself. Look as I might, I didn't recognize Babs Cantelon or Daph Lautrec, but I saw again the clothes those "flappers" wore to school the year they were "trying part of grade ten".

I had my first historical perspective of the tremendous changes that had taken place in that small community, beginning before I was born and continuing during the years that I was there, and of the changes that were still operating. Nothing stands still. While I was growing up, however, I had been much too young, too much a part of Minby to realize the significance. Remember, too, that Minby was fifteen years older than I . . .

Before Mr. Gottselig had his own threshing outfit, for instance, his threshing, like countless other farmers', was custom done at "so much a bushel," or "so much a day," by someone more enterprising or more willing than he to go into debt to buy an outfit. Generally speaking the Americans owned the big threshing outfits. Old Jack Smythe, too, became one such entrepreneur. Unfortunately, pictures from the earliest days were lacking. Maybe Gottseligs didn't have enough money for a camera at that time. Or perhaps Magdalena (she was the one who snapped all the pictures) was too young to take them. There was nevertheless a picture from 'nineteen, right after the war, with the biggest threshing outfit ever to be seen in the Minby district. It was spread out in one long thin line with all the bundle wagons, horses and men required to operate it, down to the cook cars and the women who worked around the clock to feed the enormous crew. It had been taken on the Gottselig home quarter although the outfit didn't belong to them. This threshing gang was really and truly a small empire with Old Jack Smythe fresh out of the army, master of it all. He was standing with his right hand on the flywheel of the big steamer, as proud of his most recent acquisition as if he had really bought and paid for it.

Then two other pictures, one nine or ten years later, showed Gottselig's own threshing outfit. It was the little 22-inch separator they purchased when they quit horses and bought their first tractor. Even they had time to do some custom threshing once their own and ours was finished. Magdalena pointed me out perched up on the bundle wagon that was waiting to unload. This particular picture showed the Gottselig gang, and it didn't seem to be even half the size of the Jack Smythe super-crew from 1919. The other picture, taken right in the midst of the "dirty thirties" showed the identical threshing machine, but without any hired outside help running it. The Gottselig boys, with Magdalena giving a hand, had done all their own threshing that year. They cut what grain could be salvaged with the binder as usual, but with a box mounted where the bundle carrier should have been. There was no binder twine bought that year, the wheat simply wasn't long enough to tie. When they had gathered a big enough stack of this short stuff they would start up the tractor and threshing machine, run them just long enough to thresh that pile before starting another. Those years were so lean that they considered themselves lucky when they got their seed back. There were a few years when they didn't . . .

I had the picture of the big Smythe threshing crew, then the two Gottselig pictures with the smaller gang and I began to think of what I had seen that very afternoon at Jack Fender's place. Jack was the first in Minby with one of the little John Deere combines which he operated entirely alone from his tractor. It looked like an oversized frog . . . It took a bit of time yet it could perform the task once done by a gang the size of Smythe's. The other larger combines with one man on the machine, another running the tractor, had made their appearance in Minby a few summers previously of course. Gottseligs even had a couple of them when I was there but strangely enough had no pictures of them in their collection. No wonder, then, there hadn't been harvest help from "down East"! It was Jack Fender, too, who drove me over to Gottseligs in his one-ton truck with a load of grain, and I swore that his vehicle ran as quietly and as smoothly as a car. The country roads were even better than the main road used to be between Minby and Missenden.

We passed one team and met another, each pulling wagons; but for each of these teams we met a dozen trucks throwing back dust at us as they sped by.

I wasn't in Minby too long that first time, but the talk I had with Mr. Roberts at the old Viggo garage, gave me much to digest. I was surprised to find our name still painted across the front of it.

"Why change it?" he asked, even if he was now the sole proprietor and had been for almost ten years.

Mr. Roberts couldn't complain about the living he was making. Of course he was the kind of person who would always get along. He had seen the handwriting on the wall just as my Dad had, and could have pulled out too. He had been quite satisfied to remain where he was.

"I chose Minby, Wally," he said quietly, and I remembered the first time I saw him in my Dad's old shop . . .

I learned that day, for the first time, that it was only because Mr. Roberts had stayed on in the community and had taken over the business, that my Dad had been able to make the move to B.C. when he did.

There had been lots more changes in Minby. First one machine agency and then another had withdrawn their dealership from Mr. Roberts. Old Stewart lost the B.A. Oil Agency too. That left Minby with no machine dealers where there had once been several.

"For perfectly justifiable reasons," Mr. Roberts added as if anticipating my question. "The companies are now concentrating on a few scattered well-stocked agencies in the larger points. Our boys have to go to Culbertson or Missenden, or Rottingdean or clear into the city now!"

The population of Minby itself remained fairly constant for a while even though stores were closing and the smaller farm operations ceasing to exist. That was because a number of the remaining old-timers moved into town to get away from the lonesome winter on the farm, but even more were going to Missenden to get away from the lonesome winter in Minby . . . The surviving Lobb sister moved to Missenden too. She didn't count on getting sick, but she thought it would be nice to be handy to the hospital if it were ever necessary.

"That'll be the frosty Friday when Christina Lobb leaves her Manwarin' Manor to go to Missenden," Jack Fender said at the time.

Christina didn't leave it, she paid out a small fortune to have her big house, all three stories of it, moved up to Missenden.

A few of the farmers had the last of their children in High School. With nothing beyond Grade Eight in Minby, that was one more reason to choose Missenden instead of Minby when they left the farm. Missenden had had electric lights for years. The added attraction now: they were putting in water!

One bit of information concerning Minby was given a terrific write-up in *The Western Producer* and was reprinted in every major paper across Canada. The feature dealt with the abandonment of the rail line. Without trains, elevators aren't of much use . . . The news item in question was about a line company's decision to move its elevator sixty-five miles to another point rather than build a new one. The picture in the *Producer* showed how the stupendous operation had been carried out.

Other bits of news about the old home town were the result of two chance contacts one evening when I was traveling East, both coincidences. I had to wait two hours in the city for my bus when whom should I run into but old Mrs. Cantelon from Minby. I should have said "from Missenden" because that's where she's living now. I would have recognized her had I seen her first but she with her sharp eyes was the one to first spot me.

"You're your Dad all over, Wally — I'd know you *anywheres,*" said Mrs. Cantelon.

Mrs. Cantelon brought me up to date with news about people I'm afraid I didn't even know, second generation people, third generation as well, assuming that I was as familiar with them as she was herself. She mentioned among other things that her husband had passed away the year before.

"And old Dr. Grenz looked after him, right to the last, Wally, the dear old soul! He'll never retire, Wally, that man! Why he's over seventy. It's really *too* bad, Wally, you know he doesn't *believe* . . . And yet-he's such a good doctor. Do you *really* think a good man like that will go to hell?"

After I said good-bye to Mrs. Cantelon, who should get off the very bus I was to get on but *Reverend* William Schurk, turned-back collar, looking very "dobbinair" in his dark suit. Somehow, in retrospect, the collar suited him best that way. There shouldn't have been the least doubt at all about those big teeth, that mighty jaw, that *chevaline* profile, but it was he, "Horseface" Schurk, "Alkali" Willie, who had recognized me. Oh to have just had half an hour to reminisce over Bible School days! Would he have recalled "playing threshing machine" behind the Old Stone School? or my ineffectual attempts to help him learn his catechism? The special privileges he had enjoyed at camp flashed through me mind . . .

We didn't have time to exchange more than a few words when I had to get aboard — but I promised to call in on the way back. I have his address. His invitation, however, I will keep in *special* reserve. Someday when I'm positive that my T.V. set has nothing more to offer, someday when I'm just as positively convinced that I've seen and heard *everything*, then I might just lock up the pumps some weekend and make the trip over to his town and hear one of his sermons.

Wouldn't *that* be something?